CHURCH ETIQUETTE

THE

NECESSITY OF A LEADER

BRIAN D. BEVERLY II

Church Etiquette: The Necessity of a Leader

Published by Outpour Press LLC
P.O. 4014
Hammond, LA 70404

Copyright © 2023 Brian D. Beverly II

ISBN-13: 978-1-961152-00-7

Printed in the USA

Edited by Amanda Beverly

DEDICATION

For my wife Amanda, who has been one of my greatest inspirations. You are the love of my life and I am eternally grateful for you.

For my children, Kamden, Ada, Bailey, Micaiah, and my fifth child, yet to be born. You are God's gifts to me and your mother.

For the Church of the Lord Jesus Christ! May the Church continue to push back the darkness.

CONTENTS

Each chapter builds upon another. Please read each chapter in order starting with the introduction.

INTRODUCTION

Have you ever visited a church and wondered, where do I sit? Have I dressed appropriately? Am I speaking in a God-honoring way? Is this church okay with my children staying in the adult service? Will my gifts be accepted here? Within what theological framework is this church operating? How does this church view the Holy Spirit? Are they going to start speaking in tongues? Are demons going to manifest in the service? Am I allowed to partake in communion? Questions like these, among many others, can make a person's visit to a church for the first time awkward or stressful. Even those that are regular members of churches may not fully understand their church's etiquette. And while these types of questions are necessary, the sense of fear or stress that accompanies such questions should not be.

Typically, when people attempt to understand the etiquette of the church they are visiting or belong to, they turn to a few avenues:

Statement of faith and other documents: Many churches have their faith and conduct listed somewhere on their website, visitors' packets, published books, or documentation that gives specific instructions for certain events. Some churches will have new members' classes to give newcomers a cursory overview. However, what is written on paper is sometimes different than what is practiced. Every church can state somewhere in its literature that "we are a church of vibrant worship," but how that worship looks in practice may vary from church to church. While looking at a church's documentation is a start, it still does not fully articulate a church's etiquette.

Other believers: Ideally, Christians of the same church would operate with identical faith and conduct. But looking towards other members to understand how to conduct themselves in a church setting could be problematic for many reasons.

1. Some may only be long-term visitors who do not reflect the mission of the said church.

2. Others may be new Christians who are still maturing in the sanctification process. So their language, behavior, and overall spiritual maturity may not reflect what a given church believes and practices.

3. Some members are indifferent, which means that these members have not submitted to the style, structure, and order of a given church. These types of members are not disappointed or upset with their church; they just do not have the requisite passion or activity within their church that is representative of those that understand the church's mission.

4. Still, others may be unconverted people that have yet to commit to Christ. And therefore, do not adequately portray a church's etiquette.

The truth is that protocol or etiquette differs from church to church. And one has to ask the question, why is this? In one sense, every genuine church founded upon the Lordship of Jesus Christ should have faith and practice that reflects the same Christ we profess. There are objective truths that every church must adhere to, or it is not a Christian church. But assuming that a church's doctrine is faithful to biblical scripture, the question remains: "What makes church etiquette differ between churches?"

One could conclude that it depends on the region. For example, some churches in mild weather climates may believe members should be dressed in formal wear (men in suits and women in dresses). However, there may be other climates worldwide where church members meet outside, and it is too hot to wear a full suit. Either way, so long as a person is fully clothed, what matters is if one's heart posture towards God is worshipful. Yet we know each church has a sense of clothing, music, and procedures that best articulate worship to God. So long as sound doctrine is not violated, church etiquette, stylistically and administrated pragmatically, can look different.

However, the main reason church etiquette changes between churches is because of the leader God chooses. If one wants to understand the faith and conduct of any church, all one has to do is look at the leader God put in place. Each leader is a different expression of Christ's nature and the mission Christ wants to accomplish through a given church, region, or assignment. For example, when the Israelites were under Moses' leadership, they still had a slave mentality of survival. And Moses had to die in the wilderness with an entire generation of Israelites who could not overcome their past. But once Joshua took over, he propelled a new generation of Israelites into the promised land and made them conquering warriors under his leadership. Same God, but two different kinds of leaders!

The Apostle Paul was called to the Gentiles and did not struggle to embrace that calling. But even though the Apostle Peter had a revelation of salvation coming to the Gentiles (Acts 10), he still struggled with that idea. So while Paul fully embraced the ministry to the Gentiles, at times, Peter would pretend that he did not relate to Gentiles to satisfy Jewish customs (Galatians 2:11-21).

So long as Christ was central, Paul could connect with many people. So his view on church etiquette did not have to involve all the traditions that would attract Jewish believers.

Therefore, etiquette is dependent upon the type of leader one has. Ultimately, Jesus is our Shepherd, but He gives us leaders after Christ's heart to help His people in their obedience and devotion towards Himself.

Whether you are a mainline traditional church, a charismatic church, a non-denominational church, or any other style of authentic Christian practice, this book aims to clarify why church leadership is vital to advancing God's kingdom on the earth. And I hope that Church leaders will be encouraged to lead their congregations with boldness, compassion, integrity, and absolute devotion to Christ.

Leaderless Christianity is aimless Christianity. God has designed His Church to have leaders. Please keep an open and teachable spirit as you read. And Hopefully, by the end of this book, all of us will come to a greater understanding and appreciation of church etiquette and why church leadership is so important.

CHAPTER ONE

THE KINGDOM

The most powerful message ever heard around the world is the gospel of Jesus Christ. The central message of Christianity is that God's Son died for the sins of humanity. God is a holy and righteous judge, and sin cannot go unpunished. Sin is defiance of the King. If God does not punish sin/defiance, His rule is not absolute. To maintain His throne, God must punish disobedience. And yet, God is a loving Father. He delights in showing mercy (Micah 7:18). He is faithful to His creation, hallelujah! Therefore, He chose to punish the One for the redemption of the many. Christ took our punishment for us. The ministry of Christ is the clear demonstration of the wrath and justice of God, intertwined with His love and mercy. When one trusts in the sacrifice of Christ, he or she is saved and becomes a legitimate child of God. If there was only one message to preach, the gospel of Christ is that message. The simple gospel message is more important than sermons on finances, marriage, spiritual gifts, denominational/associational goals, or other topics.

This message was enough to save a thief who was dying on a cross. And while Christians should be baptized by the water and the Spirit, this thief was not even baptized by either—and Christ still saved him. Notice what the thief had said: "*Jesus, remember me when you come into your kingdom*" (Luke 23:42, NIV). Christ granted his request. Interestingly, the thief had some idea about Christ's kingdom. Whether the thief's thoughts were complete or limited about Christ's kingdom, he knew there must have been an empire backing Him. This kingdom was more significant than his present circumstance. Otherwise, he would have only asked for Christ to save his physical life. No, he sensed that salvation was part of an empire to which Jesus would escort him! What one needs to understand is that salvation is only the beginning! It is the entry point to His kingdom.

Jesus talked a lot about the kingdom. He claimed that the gospel was an extension of His domain. He said, "...*I must proclaim the good news of the kingdom of God to the other towns also, because that is why I was sent*" (Luke 4:43). Jesus said the gospel is "of" or "from" the kingdom. Therefore, the gospel is the front door that leads to more of the kingdom—it is the beginning. John the Baptist, the forerunner for Jesus, told people to repent of their sins because the kingdom was near (Matthew 3:2). John understood that repentance was necessary to enter the kingdom. Jesus taught His disciples to pray for the kingdom to come on the earth (Matthew 6:10). He claimed that the kingdom existed within us (Luke 17:21). He gave earthly examples to explain His kingdom symbolically. When Jesus cast out a demon, He directly stated that it was a result of the kingdom (Matthew 12:28). Many people claimed that Jesus was a king, and Jesus did not deny it. Why? Because He is the King of His kingdom. Christianity is more than just being saved and attending church; there is a kingdom.

Imagine a person struggling to swim in the open sea. This individual is about to drown. Just before his arms and legs give out, someone rescues the person in a lifeboat. After getting to safety, what should be the immediate response of the person who was saved? Would the person critically analyze the one who rescued his life? Would one demand to see the credentials of the one who preserved his life? Or would it be more appropriate for the person to respond in gratitude to the one that saved his life? Simply put, a person saved moments from death would be immensely grateful to his hero. The "how" or "why" would not matter as much compared to the overwhelming joy of having one's life saved.

The same is true of the Christian experience. Yes, Christians need to understand their salvation; there is a faithful and intellectual approach people can have toward Christianity. Nonetheless, when people spend most of their time at the "front door" of Christianity, attempting to understand their salvation, they could miss out on the "more than" that the kingdom offers.

The disciples did not understand everything about Christ and the type of salvation He was bringing. They did, however, drop their nets and follow Him (Matthew 4:20). The man who was once lame could not explain to the pharisees how Christ healed him, but he was grateful to be healed (John 5:8-13). Peter could not explain "how" or "why" Christ walked on water, but he did walk on water like Jesus did (Matthew 14:22-33). In other words, only some ideas can be explained, and other concepts must be experienced.

How did the Apostle Paul get saved? Did he pray for Christ to come into his heart? No, Christ interrupted his life on the road to Damascus. From there, Paul began to follow God. He only had to explain or teach the faith later in order to lead people to an encounter with God through evangelism and discipleship. Paul did an incredible job of explaining salvation to the Romans because they had yet to have an experience with Christ. In other words, Paul understood that words or teaching alone would not save a person—one would need to encounter Christ. Paul states: "*For the kingdom of God is not a matter of talk but of power*" (1 Corinthians 4:20). People absolutely need to hear the gospel preached as scripture states. But if the preaching does not lead to an encounter with God, it could simply be a motivational speech. Before converting, Paul had heard many viewpoints about Jesus. And all the ideas he heard caused Paul to hunt Christians in order to persecute them.

Fortunately, his pursuit led him to a radical experience with Christ that caused him to address Christ as "Lord" (Acts 9:3-5). The kingdom is so important to Jesus that after He rose from the dead, He spent forty days teaching His disciples about the kingdom (Acts 1:3). Interestingly, the kingdom was what Jesus told people to seek first (Matthew 6:33). Hence, God does not just save people for them to overanalyze their salvation and wait idly for His return. Once again, salvation is only the starting place or the entrance to His kingdom.

Church etiquette is important because we are citizens of Christ's kingdom. How people conduct themselves in the King's domain will make one a citizen or a traitor. God always fulfills His will and not someone else's. He supports His Kingdom, not ours. An attempt to have a kingdom outside God's will is to become like Satan. While it would take another book to talk about the kingdom of God thoroughly, we at least have to understand something about the kingdom to appreciate church etiquette. What follows in the coming sections and chapters will be sufficient for your understanding of God's kingdom for this book's purpose.

RULE AND REIGN/SOVEREIGNTY

It is not an under or overstatement to say that God rules and reigns! His authority and His power are absolute. God has no competitor. He has never felt insecure, incomplete, insufficient, or compromised. While He is the beginning and end of all time, He had no origin story—He existed before the creation of time. No place on earth or within the universe is unknown to God. He fills all space and matter. Whatever direction one may go, God's signature is everywhere. Even hell is God's creation. Hence, in its simplest form, the kingdom of God is about a sovereign and eternal King whose rule and reign have no beginning or end. It is an everlasting kingdom because God is immortal.

Therefore if someone were to ask, "When did God's kingdom start?" the answer would be that His kingdom has been present for as long as He has existed. When Moses wanted to know the name of the Lord, God told Moses that "*I AM WHO I AM...*" (Exodus 3:14). In other words, God "IS." We do call Him Jehovah because that is in the Bible. But what is compelling is that God frequently allowed people to address Him based on their experience of Him. David spoke of God as his "Rock" and "Fortress" (Psalm 18:2). Abraham referenced God as his "Provider" (Genesis 22:14). The matter concludes that God "IS." He is everything, and without Him, there is nothing! Therefore, He "IS" everything we experience Him to be, but He is not limited to our experience. Neither can He be reduced to any blasphemous names the rebellious and uninitiated attempt to place on God.

More importantly, the name of God that is above all other names is Jesus! It is by the name of Jesus we are saved (Philippians 2:9). In the name of Jesus is the fullness of God (Colossians. 2:9). Demons tremble at that name. The name of Jesus only becomes superstitious and powerless when one does not understand the person behind the name. During biblical times, some people saw Jesus and only thought of Him as a carpenter, a Nazarene, or a rabbi. However, the Christian invokes the name of Jesus, knowing He was and is God. And His kingdom follows after His name and no one other—the kingdom is the expressed will of Jesus, which is conveyed in a local church since Jesus is the head of the Church (Colossians 1:18).

Christ is supreme regardless if one agrees or not. There is coming a day when all beings will acknowledge His supremacy: The Bible says, "*...at the name of Jesus every knee should bow, in heaven and on earth and under the earth, and every tongue acknowledges that Jesus Christ is Lord, to the glory of God the*

Father" (Philippians 2:10-11). The kingdom requires people to acknowledge the absolute rule and reign of Jesus Christ!

VISIBLE GOVERNMENT

In some ways, God's kingdom is invisible. However, there are people like Isaiah, Ezekiel, and the Apostle John who saw the throne room of God. There is imagery in the Bible of angels, streets of gold, vivid colors, and music. In the end, Christ returns as a conquering King descending from this kingdom. God's kingdom exists in the spiritual realm. But it is also visible in that disciples are to display kingdom character through the fruit of the Spirit and demonstrate the kingdom's power. So there is an invisible kingdom yet to be known. What can be known currently is what the Christian is commissioned to reveal to the world. The following will highlight the visible kingdom of God on earth.

Government: God has commissioned governing leaders called fivefold ministers (apostles, prophets, evangelists, pastors, and teachers). There are also bishops, elders, and deacons. And while every fivefold minister must meet the qualifications of an elder, only some elders are fivefold ministers. For example, Moses was the fivefold minister (governing and senior prophet). However, he had seventy elders to help him make spiritual decisions (Numbers 11:16-17). Deacons serve the practical needs of the people both spiritually and physically (Acts 6:1-7). Furthermore, there are workers of ministry, which means that every Christian is called to do some ministry for the Church/world. There are visible positions of different ranks and responsibilities representing God's kingdom on earth.

Warfare: Every kingdom needs an army. Scripture teaches that we have an enemy called the Devil. This battle is spiritual but does have an impact on the physical. There is armor (Ephesians 6:11), weapons (2 Corinthians 10:4), and a militant disposition the believer must have to overcome this life (2 Timothy 2:4).

Economy: Like any government or society, there is an economic system. Monetary gain is necessary for God's visible kingdom on earth. Moreover, it could be explored that the kingdom's currency includes topics of faith, hope, love, honor, and the like. Indeed, God prospered people throughout scripture because they acted on these virtues. For instance, one can only please God by faith, and one must come in faith when asking God for things. One cannot receive anything from God without faith (James 1:6-8). There are other forms of prosperity that are not limited to money, but it would take another book to discuss those various levels of spiritual currency.

However, we will focus on kingdom finances since God has established biblical principles to bless us financially. In short, poverty is evil. It produces physical hunger, causes people to become criminals, and strips humanity of their dignity. The child who will starve tonight would not call poverty a blessing. Therefore God will raise kingdom financiers who enjoy the wealth God has given them but will also use it for others. God made Abraham wealthy and a blessing to many (Genesis 13:2,12:2). Chapter seven will be dedicated primarily to the discussion of money, because there is much confusion on this topic.

Legislation: Jesus gave Peter the keys to the kingdom. As a result, he could bind and loose things, and heaven would authorize what he decreed (Matthew 16:19). This authority is restrained to God's will. Nonetheless, binding and loosing have a sense of legality to them. Even Job stated that a righteous person could decree something and it would be established or legalized (Job 22:28). Adam was given a charge to name the animals. What he decreed from his mouth became the fact of the matter. Some animals were called camels, dogs, or elephants because Adam named them and God affirmed/legalized them. One may speak within the bounds and sovereignty of God's kingdom, and it becomes legislation! Elijah prayed to God that it would not rain, and when he said it, the rain did not fall for three and a half years (James 5:17, 1 Kings 17:1).

Typically speaking, when people think about the laws of God, they think about the ten commandants or love. Primarily because Jesus talked about how all the law rested on the command to love God and your neighbor (Matthew 22:40). Love saves and brings us into the kingdom. From that love, we begin legislating and advancing God's kingdom by decreeing, declaring, and establishing. In other words, why pray if one does not believe God acts in the world?

Marketplace and governmental influence: Joseph influenced the marketplace and government of Egypt. Without Joseph's marketplace and administrative insight, Egypt and Israel would have starved during a famine. Daniel had an impact on the Babylonian government. The prophets of the Old Testament would advise kings. Paul was a tent maker and spoke to kings like Agrippa (Acts 26). The advancement of God's kingdom extends to the secular marketplaces and governments (Acts 17:17).

* There is more that could be said about the Kingdom of God. This section has served as an introduction to the kingdom so that you may better understand church etiquette.

OUR RESPONSE TO THE KINGDOM

Once the Christian understands and embraces that there is a visible kingdom of God, then what should our response be?

Surely the contemporaries of Christ did not understand the kingdom He was trying to introduce. Many thought Jesus' rule would be militant as David's was. They were waiting for Christ to liberate them from Roman occupation, as God had delivered them from previous pagan governments. Optimistically I want to believe that modern Christians will not make the same mistake as they did in the gospel narratives. God's kingdom is more significant than any political party, skin color, economic status, or country. Christ is the God of all nations, even though some do not recognize Him as such. He does require a response to His Lordship. Especially since one day, He will judge the world (Revelation 20). Until then, let us consider what our response should be:

Obedience: Jesus is a benevolent king. He healed, fed, financially provided, and taught the multitudes. In the end, none of the people Christ had graciously helped spoke up on His behalf. Despite all the miracles before their eyes, they chose Barabbas over Jesus (Luke 23:18). The apostles He trained in three years deserted Him. People watched idly by as He was sent to the cross. He served those He knew would betray Him. And yet, when He rose from the dead, He still gave eternal life to those that believed in Him.

What Jesus requires of us is belief! If one genuinely believes in Jesus, one will be obedient toward Him and His kingdom. Will one do everything right? No! Christ made provision for when Christians make a mistake or wrong choice (1 John 1:9). The faithful Christian repents and continues to follow Jesus while making His kingdom known. As Christians, we love God because we know that He loves us. It is the Christian's constant desire to be obedient to Jesus when you truly love Him (1 Peter 1:8). The true believer finds joy in obedience to our Lord.

Advancement: When speaking about the kingdom, Jesus stated that one is not suited for His kingdom if one keeps looking back to one's past life (Luke 9:62). The kingdom is constantly advancing. One must find his or her mission for advancing God's kingdom. One's mission could be the fivefold ministry, the marketplace, or simply committing to raise godly children who understand God's kingdom. Once saved, Christians should ask themselves: "God, what are you telling me to do for your kingdom?"

When John the Baptist was in prison and inquiring about the identity of Jesus, Christ sent this message to him: "*The blind receive sight, the lame walk, those who have leprosy are cleansed, the deaf hear, the dead are raised, and the good news is proclaimed to the poor*" (Matthew 11:5). John needed to know that the kingdom he preached about, while in the wilderness, was advancing. The signs, wonders, miracles, and the gospel proclaimed were the signifiers that God's kingdom was upon them. And this kingdom was indeed setting people free from their spiritual, mental, and physical ailments. In other words, the kingdom advanced beyond John's ministry and would continue to increase. We must endeavor to understand and act out our role in His kingdom.

ECCLESIA

Now that we have a general understanding of the kingdom of God, we must grasp how the kingdom interacts with His church. As alluded to in the previous section, "Rule And Reign/ Sovereignty," the kingdom of God has always existed before time. Before there was a Church (assembly of God's people), there was a kingdom with a King. The kingdom comes before the Church. Without the kingdom, there would be no Church. While the Church is a place to worship God and enjoy the fellowship of like-minded believers, King Jesus also meant for it to be an embassy representing kingdom ambitions. When one looks at the original meaning and intent of the word "church," we gain a better understanding of how the Church is to function.

The Greek word "ecclesia" is translated to "church" in the Bible. It simply means "called out ones." These are people that are called out to convene. In its more straightforward understanding, the word means "assembly" or "gathering." Before this word became associated with the Christian Church, this "assembly" gathered for another purpose. An ecclesia in ancient Greece was a council that would congregate to make decisions concerning legislation, military strategy, declarations of war, and would handle civil disputes. They would gather with the intentionality of advancing the Greek way of life.

Biblically speaking, the way an ecclesia conducted itself in the Greco-Roman world can be seen in Acts 19:23-41. Herein is a scene that takes place with an ecclesia present. Verse 32 states, *"The assembly was in confusion."* The word translated to assembly in this verse is the Greek word ecclesia. The confusion resulted from the people shouting disorderly because they were upset with the Apostle Paul's preaching. His message was negatively affecting their businesses and blaspheming their gods. So an ecclesia was called in for a civil matter.

The ancient Greeks would gather to keep order and advance Greek influence. Likewise, God's Church (ecclesia) is meant to assemble to maintain order and advance His kingdom. The Church has governors (fivefold ministers), legislation (spiritual decrees and intercession), and spiritual warfare/military strategy; among other things we have mentioned in this chapter.

Upon having this knowledge of the "ecclesia," one must ask themselves: "Does the Church at large fit the historical and original intent of the word ecclesia? Are we advancing God's agenda or our own? Are we making churches in our image or His image?" And because the kingdom backs the Church, Christians should display etiquette representative of the kingdom to which they belong.

HARMONY/PEACE

Pain is always the result of a disorder. When someone's limbs are broken, there will be pain because the body is out of order. When a person's immune system is compromised, he or she will be more susceptible to illness. If the street lights directing traffic are faulty, that could cause car wrecks. Likewise, any church or ministry in disorder will be filled with rebellion and strife. Wherever there is disorder, there will be chaos and pain accompanying it.

Distilling chaos is why the governments of the world exist. It is an attempt to bring order to chaos. However, people have selfish ambitions with goals that are not always benevolent. People are fallible. Consequently, earthly governments are never pure, they get toppled, and some become tyrannical. Nonetheless, the best examples of worldly governments provide structure, order, and a sense of stability, even though it is not perfect.

The imperfections of our worldly governments should cause us to see God's kingdom not as an alternative but as the way it ought to be. And while, as God's children, we will struggle to get it right every time, God's kingdom is the best and only way to govern His church. The world has its governments, and we have His kingdom—we are kingdom citizens.

So when Christ told those early believers to make disciples, He was not limiting it to salvation and the intricacies of how one is saved. Instead, He was talking about His kingdom. As you continue in the pages ahead, this book will have a kingdom approach. It will attempt to bring the kingdom view of structure and order to the church—this structure and order is known as etiquette.

CHAPTER TWO

THE VISIONARY LEADER

One of the reoccurring themes in the Bible is that whenever God's people were in trouble or in need of direction, the Lord would raise a man or woman to deliver His people. God raised Abraham to be the father of many and Moses to deliver God's people from bondage. God established leaders known as "Judges" or rulers to defend His people (Judges 2:16), judges like Ehud, Jephthah, Deborah, Gideon, Samson, and the like. God established His apostles —"sent ones" to advance His kingdom and lead His people. Even the book of Hebrews has an entire chapter dedicated to acknowledging great leaders God raised (Hebrews 11). After having commemorated all these heroes of the faith, I love the way the writer of Hebrews concludes chapter eleven:

And what more shall I say? I do not have time to tell about Gideon, Barak, Samson and Jephthah, about David and Samuel and the prophets, who through faith conquered kingdoms, administered justice, and gained what was promised; who shut the mouths of lions, quenched the fury of the flames, and escaped the edge of the sword; whose weakness was turned to strength; and who became powerful in battle and routed foreign armies. Women received back their dead, raised to life again. There were others who were tortured, refusing to be released so that they might gain an even better resurrection. Some faced jeers and flogging, and even chains and imprisonment. They were put to death by stoning; they were sawed in two; they were killed by the sword. They went about in sheepskins and goatskins, destitute, persecuted and mistreated— the world was not worthy of them. They wandered in deserts and mountains, living in caves and in holes in the ground. (32-38)

Without a doubt, the writer of this book cherishes the memory of these great leaders. He recalls the mighty power of God working through people. In other words, throughout history, God has always worked through anointed men and women. God designates a visionary leader. And while there may be others in leadership to provide support, there is a leader among the leaders to set the pace for everyone to follow.

Moses was distinguished from other leaders. Part of his leadership team consisted of two different prophets (Exodus 7:1, Exodus 15:20). His brother Aaron and his sister Miriam were both prophets. But Moses was the visionary leader among them in that God spoke differently to Moses than how God spoke to the other prophets, or anyone else that would come and support Moses' leadership. Notice the reprimand God gave to Aaron and Miriam when they became competitive with Moses:

...When there is a prophet among you, I, the Lord, reveal myself to them in visions, I speak to them in dreams. But this is not true of my servant Moses; he is faithful in all my house. With him I speak face to face, clearly and not in riddles; he sees the form of the Lord. Why then were you not afraid to speak against my servant Moses? The anger of the Lord burned against them, and he left them. (Numbers 12:6-9)

God wanted the ministry team to know that while they were all prophets, Moses was still set apart as the visionary leader. God spoke and revealed things to Moses that he was to transmit to others. It becomes contradictory to the Word of God when people claim to not need leadership or to be their leader's equal. God, in His wisdom, selects a leader to govern (Jeremiah 3:15).

THE ANOINTING

Sometimes we talk about anointing without understanding what it means. The anointing implies designation, which means that someone or something has been set apart by God for His glory and purposes. Some might assume if one prophesies, heals the sick, or speaks in tongues, then that person must be anointed. But just because someone is gifted does not mean that person is anointed. Bullies can also be powerful and gifted. And most people have met gifted and powerful bullies! No doubt, Goliath was a powerful bully gifted with strength but he had no designation from God.

Conversely, David acknowledged that as an Israelite, he was anointed to defeat Goliath. A sign of God's covenant with Israel was circumcision. David, being a circumcised Israelite, was convinced he would defeat Goliath. And he did. Because of God's covenant, he could not lose to the uncircumcised giant (1 Samuel 17:36).

Pharaoh and his magicians were bullies who had power! His sorcerers, like Moses, could do great signs and wonders but were not anointed like Moses. (Exodus 7:8-13). Simon, the sorcerer, had great power but was not anointed as the apostles were (Acts 8:9-25). It is possible to have power without being anointed. However, you cannot be anointed without having authority (designation from God).

The anointing has to do with the authority given based on the assignment or place of jurisdiction. For example, people have the authority and power to redecorate their homes as they see fit. But a modification to a house that is not your own is called vandalism. While you have the power to do it, you are not authorized to do so. Hence, it becomes a crime.

The visionary leader of a church house is the one authorized by Christ to delegate and make the final decision. The people under the leader may be anointed and have power, but only as it relates to the visionary leader. Consider how Aaron's prophetic function was connected to Moses' leadership: "*Then the Lord said to Moses, 'See, I have made you like God to Pharaoh, and your brother **Aaron will be your prophet**. You are to say everything I command you, and your brother Aaron is to tell Pharaoh to let the Israelites go out of his country*'" (Exodus 7:1-2, emphasis mine). Moses believed he was not a gifted communicator. So God made his brother Aaron a prophet to assist Moses in public speaking. Therefore, Aaron's office as a prophet was only as necessary as it was in helping Moses fulfill his role as the visionary leader. Without Moses, there would be no need for Aaron's ministry as a prophet—they complement each other. They are both needed to fulfill God's plan. Was Aaron authoritative? Yes! But his authority was in support of and not to supersede Moses.

A church must understand that they have a visionary leader because God chose him or her. Is the visionary leader flawless? Certainly, visionary leaders such as Father Abraham, King David, Apostle Peter, and the like had flaws. However, they got the job done. God does not make mistakes. The visionary leader God chooses cannot be replaced or voted out by an ungodly consensus. This leader can only be disqualified if he or she fails to follow the Lord's commands. But hopefully, one will see throughout this book that leaders are necessary.

KEY CARRIERS

In the gospel of Luke chapter four, Jesus quotes the Prophet Isaiah concerning his anointing. He states, "*The Spirit of the Lord is on me, because he has anointed me to proclaim good news to the poor. He has sent me to proclaim freedom for the prisoners and recovery of sight for the blind, to set the oppressed free, to proclaim the year of the Lord's favor"* (18-19).

Pay attention to the order of the passage. First, Jesus claimed to be anointed because God's Spirit was on Him (Jesus is designated). Second, Jesus made it very clear that His designation comes with the power to "proclaim," bring "recovery," secure "freedom," and establish "favor." Jesus was not anointed for show but for action. A direct result of the anointing upon His life was that He had the keys to set people free!

Whenever someone came in contact with Jesus, one could be confident that his or her life would be changed. One could be a blind man on the side of the road crying out for Jesus to restore his sight and be healed (Luke 18:35-43). A prominent pharisee inquiring of Jesus at night who became confounded by His wisdom (John 3:1-15). Or a crowd of 5,000 hungry people who witnessed the supernatural multiplication of fish and loaves of bread (Matthew 14:13-21). If one is anointed, that one will have a significant impact. Such was the case with Jesus and is the case with any visionary leader Jesus selects.

Visionary leaders are not easily replaced because they have specific keys to unlock the success needed for the body of Christ. The military commander Naaman would have remained leprous had he not asked for Elisha's help (2 Kings 5). A barren woman would have remained childless if Elisha had not prayed (2 Kings 4:16). Military campaigns would have been lost without the strategic minds of Deborah, Joshua, or Jehu. A paralyzed man would have begged for money at a temple gate his whole life if Peter and John did not command his healing (Acts 3:1-10). The Church would not have a record of the life of Jesus had not leaders written it down. God chooses and gives specific leaders keys for the freedom of others.

No doubt Peter was an influential key-carrying apostle. One day Jesus asked His disciples about who people thought He was. And while there was much speculation concerning His identity, only Peter was the one to know His true identity. Then Jesus changed his name from Simon to Peter and said, "*I will give you the keys of the kingdom of heaven...*" (Matthew 16:19a).

In one sense, what Jesus said to Peter is what Jesus said to His Church. Nonetheless, this was directly spoken to Peter. And as a result of his promotion, Peter had unique access to kingdom power and influence. Peter operated in such miracle-working power that people believed his shadow could heal people (Acts 5:15).

The keys given to the visionary leader are not only for demonstrating God's power but for godly wisdom. God grants the visionary leader access to wisdom that He does not give to everybody. Noah had insight into an impending flood and how to build a ship to rescue his family and animals. Solomon was the wisest man on earth; whenever someone brought an issue to him, he had keen insight on how to solve the problem (1 Kings 3:24-28). God even claims that He does not do anything on the earth without first letting His prophets know (Amos 3:7). Visionary leaders are not optional. God establishes them for the betterment of His people and the world.

GOD PROTECTS THE OFFICE

The Bible is full of gripping narratives. One narrative that has always intrigued me is when Abraham is in Egypt in a city called Gerar. And because his wife Sarah was beautiful, Abraham feared someone would kill him to have her. So Abraham lies to King Abimelek, telling the king that Sarah is only his sister. Abimelek takes Sarah for his own, but before he consummates the relationship, God appears to Abimelek in a dream. Stating that Sarah is a married woman and that if he sleeps with her, God will kill him (Genesis 20:1-7).

While Sarah was under King Abimelek's care, his kingdom was suffering. There was an ailment Abimelek was dealing with (perhaps infertility), and all the women of his kingdom could no longer conceive while he was holding onto Sarah. However, once he released Sarah, Abraham prayed for him, and everything was restored (Genesis 20:8-18).

Abraham lied! He was clearly in the wrong! As a result, he put King Abimelek in jeopardy with God. However, even though Abraham was wrong, God made it right on his behalf. God goes directly to Abimelek and lets him know of Abraham's deceit while still making Abimelek accountable for any further action he takes. God will punish Abimelek if he continues to pursue Sarah, but what of Abraham's punishment? Does God scold Abraham? No! At least there is nothing written in the scripture of a possible reprimand.

Even though Abraham is wrong, God intervenes on Abraham's behalf and makes it right because of God's grace. Why?

1) This is primarily because of the office Abraham carries. When God communicates with King Abimelek, He purposely tells him to return Abraham's wife because he is a "prophet" (Genesis 20:7). Abraham is a unique prophet in that he is the visionary leader or the father of our faith. So even in this event, Abraham's purpose outweighs Abimelek's and must be protected. Abimelek is responsible for a country, but Abraham would become the father of many nations.

2) Because even our earthly parents saved us from trouble when we were children. Our parents or guardians took responsibility for us as their children and made things right when we were wrong. God does the same for Abraham (Romans 8:28).

Abraham is great, but not because he did everything just right. Instead, he truly believed in God, which became his righteousness (Romans 4:3)! God loves it when His people believe in Him. Abimelek only had enough faith to believe God would destroy him if he slept with Sarah. Therefore, he made the necessary changes and even blessed Abraham with an offering to make things right with God. That is where his faith ends. Abimelek could have judged Abraham for his deceit, and it would be true! Abimelek only says and does things because he does not want to get in trouble with God. But Abraham left everything to follow God! Do you see the difference? Sure, Abimelek could be right this time, but Abraham has given his entire life to God. Abraham will continue to follow God beyond his mistake. And this is what makes us Christian. Although we are not without our flaws, our flawless God continues to make intercession for us and is maturing us daily into Christlikeness as long as we continue to pursue Him.

God will remove corrupt leaders. He removed King Saul when he was corrupted. He removed King Nebuchadnezzar for a season.

But Abraham was not corrupt in his affection towards God; he just made a foolish decision. Likewise, David probably upset many people with his extramarital affair with Bathsheba and murdering her husband. Nonetheless, when confronted with his sin, David still had the heart to please God and repented immediately (Psalm 51).

Hence, God chose Able over Cain because Able's heart and affections were true toward God. God chooses visionary leaders not because they are infallible but because they genuinely pursue God. And He has placed precious cargo within a visionary leader to help His Church. Cargo that the Lord will protect. Now one understands why scripture says not to harm God's anointed people or His prophets (Psalms 105:15).

Because of the anointing God placed upon Abraham, people were blessed or cursed based on their interaction with Abraham (Genesis 12:3). According to the Old Testament, to touch the Ark of the Covenant in an irreverent way brought death (2 Samuel 6:6-7). The Ark of the Covenant was the place where God's presence dwelled. And all believers have become an "ark" of God's presence. Nonetheless, some have been anointed with a specific responsibility to help people. And God makes sure to defend His vessels.

Before Peter became a great apostle, he was a work in progress. He would speak when he should not have and even denied the Lord Jesus three times—but God chose him, and Peter became a strong leader for God. In short, regardless of whether people like the visionary leader, God made the choice! Remember, in the end, nobody seemed to like Jesus, and they put Him on the cross. But He was still the Savior. God does not raise or remove leaders because of consensus among the people. And one must understand that if a visionary leader is anointed, there is a reason for it, and God is backing that position.

When Aaron was anointed as a priest, the oil ran down his head, beard, collar, and the rest of his garments (Psalm 133:1-3). He was drenched with anointing oil. Symbolically, Aaron's anointing implies how leadership flows:

Head: Jesus is the head of the Church (Ephesians 1:22). He is the initiator. All spiritual and practical things related to the Church flow from Him, and He is the Chief of every church where He is Lord.

Beard: This word in Hebrew not only means hair related to the chin, but it derives from a Hebrew word that also means "to age" or "elder." What begins with Christ then flows to the elders of the Church (visionary leader) and other fivefold ministers (apostles, prophets, evangelists, pastors, and teachers). Notice that the beard is connected directly to the head. Hence, these are people of maturity that help lead God's people. God purposed them closer to the head (Christ) to give them direct information on guiding His people. The visionary leader and other fivefold ministers of various Christian circles can also be called "Headship gifts."

Collar/garments: And now that which started from the head, begins to flow down to the rest of the garments of the body (Romans 12:4-5). The rest of the church is anointed for service given their perspective ministries (deacon, nursery, and so on).

This is how God established leadership. It goes from Christ to His "bearded ones," or elders, to the rest of the body (congregation or workers of ministry). Notice the oil does not rise from the feet, the shins, knee caps, and up to the head—no, it begins first with the head. And this is the issue sometimes in a church. When one does not understand how leadership flows, congregational members act like the beard (elders/fivefold). Or the elders do not understand their authority and, in effect, reduce their anointing down to the congregation (garments) by refusing to lead for fear of offending people.

One must understand that as the oil flows, it begins to thin out. Christ is the anointed one, followed by His elders/fivefold ministers. So the problem is when a congregational member tries to act like an elder without being called by God, they do not have enough oil/anointing to sustain that position. This is called pastoral burnout at times! Now naturally, people can get tired. However, whenever pastors are burnt out to the extent that they despise their ministry and retire too early, it could mean they were never called to be an elder in the first place. And they could not sustain the character, fortitude, and stamina required for the position. Therefore, it is important for people to stay in their place of anointing so that the Church can continue to be productive. Then the Holy Spirit will not be grieved (Ephesians

4:30), as He beautifully and succinctly moves through this flow for His glory.

FOLLOW THE LEADER

Why is the title of this book Church Etiquette: *The Necessity of a Leader?* Because who your leader is, indicates what you will become (at least in part). The leader is the one that sets the boundaries for what is appropriate and what is not within a given local church. The entire book of James is about James addressing the congregation on how to conduct themselves in a God-honoring way. The Apostle Paul said that people should follow him, as he is following Christ (1 Corinthians 11:1). He was setting the expectations.

Paul would also say, *"Whatever you have learned or received or heard from me, or seen in me—put it into practice. And the God of peace will be with you"* (Philippians 4:9). When Paul sends his spiritual son Timothy to be of help to a church, he assures Timothy's competency by letting that church know that Timothy practiced his way of life. It was Paul's lifestyle that became his credentials (1 Corinthians 4:17). How does one learn about the life of Christ? It is through the eyes of four gospel writers and even old testament writers like Isaiah who gave prophetic imagery concerning Christ. There are things a person learns from God through a direct relationship with the Holy Spirit. But many times, the Spirit working through others produces much fruit in a person's life.

Of course, some biblical doctrines and practices always remain the same. Nonetheless, the truth is that if a person wants to know what is appropriate for any given congregation, look at the conduct and character of the visionary leader, and one will understand what is appropriate. For example, if the visionary leader is casual in nature, the church will be casual in its approach to faith and conduct. Visionary leaders who reside in

Africa may have a style of conduct different from those in the United States of America. If the visionary leader is more studious, prophetic, apostolic, outreach driven, mannerly, passionate, regal, or believes in punctuality, then the congregation will reflect some of that nature, faith, and conduct.

While each church should be the same at its core (bringing glory to Christ with a kingdom message), Christ may have each church, bringing Him glory differently. If it is not heretical, follow the leader.

CHAPTER THREE

LEADERSHIP IS GOD'S DESIGN

A ll people need and experience leadership—it is part of God's grand design. The first introduction to leadership is our parents. Even if a person did not have natural parents, he or she had some form of parental guidance (adoptive, foster parents). Parents are responsible for setting a foundation of belief and conduct for their children, leading to a relationship with God (Proverbs 22:6). Some parental figures could have raised their children poorly. Regardless of the circumstance, parents contribute to some of our patterns of thinking and behavior as we mature. There are traditions, practices, and ways of speech people pick up due to their parents.

Throughout life, we rely on leaders of all kinds to set the pace, principles, procedures, philosophy, and purpose of a given circumstance. The roads driven on, the electronic devices employed, the restaurants patronized, and the essential house utilities used are all the result of leadership. When one traces back to the origin of every invention or service created, there was a leader that started and leaders that maintained it so that people can continue to enjoy the product. Whenever something is wrong with an establishment, people ask to speak to the leader to bring a solution. There is no such thing as a "self-made" person. The very thought itself is brooding with arrogance and pride. A person's life is comprised of the ingenuity of a community (which includes leaders) and not a single person. Adam could not do life alone; therefore, God created Eve (Genesis 2:18).

God designed us to have leaders throughout life in general and in particular regarding His Church. In the Church, God has established leaders or commanding officers called apostles, prophets, evangelists, pastors, and teachers (Ephesians 4:11)—the "fivefold ministry." These ministers are ordained by God, with particular functions for the body of Christ that keeps the Church healthy in its purpose and mission. This book is not an attempt to explain each leader but to acknowledge that God has established different types of leaders necessary for His Church. (For a deeper understanding of these leaders, see my book: *Fivefold Ministry: Access Granted.*) And while there are different tiers of leadership, as mentioned in the previous chapter, God always chooses a visionary or prominent leader to carry and delegate His vision to the congregation. So whether you or your visionary leader is an apostle, pastor, and so on, let us continue to have a teachable mind as we break down what the visionary leader and fivefold leadership are meant to do in a church.

NO RESPECTER OF PERSONS

Sometimes there is a lack of honor or respect given to church leaders. This lack of decency is partly the result of false leaders who have erred to the degree of deluding the significance of the role. Nonetheless, God is the one that places people in leadership. And Christians have a right to discern if a leader is creditable or not (1 John 4:1).

Not everyone is called to church leadership! And when someone attempts to step into leadership without being chosen by God, they create division or schism in the church whether they intended to or not. While God is not a respecter of persons (Romans 2:11), God does respect or acknowledge those who make much of the grace given. Meaning that God loves us all the same, but He trusts us differently depending on the commitment necessary for the assignment. In the following are two groups with different tiers of discipleship and responsibility.

Workers of ministries: All Christians are called to participate in some form of ministry. All should be able to share their testimony of how Christ saved them. However, being a "worker of ministry" has more to do with "helping" or "assisting" than it does with governmental ministry.

Five hundredth tier: "*...he appeared to more than five hundred of the brothers and sisters at the same time, most of whom are still living, though some have fallen asleep*" (1 Corinthians 15:6). Notice that after Jesus was resurrected, He met with at least 500 believers. What were these people's names? What did they accomplish? What were their personalities? The answer is unknown. One could make assumptions about what they accomplished and who they were. But, all we know is that they were "brothers and sisters" of the faith. Yet, they were nameless and faceless.

These believers may not be the leaders of great movements, but they foster great moves of God. Just like a fire needs to be kindled, they continually promote and elevate the cause of Christ and fill in where needed. These people are more recognized for their enthused commitment than their giftedness and collective influence instead of being celebrated as individuals. For example, the Apostle Peter had an incredible ministry. But part of what made his ministry so impactful was the committed prayer ministry supporting him.

One time Peter was in prison awaiting trial. Potentially he could have received a death sentence. But he never made his court date because the "...church was earnestly praying to God for him" (Acts 12:5). As a result of this church's prayer, an angel supernaturally freed Peter from prison.

Thank God for believers, although nameless and faceless, that commit to promoting the cause of Christ. They may be in the background, but their actions impact the foreground. And one day, God will reward these people for their sacrifices for His kingdom.

Seventieth tier: In Luke chapter ten, Jesus anoints 70 disciples (some translations say 72) to do ministry. Jesus sends them to communities to heal the sick, cast out demons, and proclaim His kingdom (1-23). At this tier, the 12 disciples were within the 70 and would be recognizable. But this group at large is still nameless and faceless. Yet, they are mighty.

This tier of 70 is for those Christians that understand they have a Christian assignment. They submit their talents and gifts to the Holy Spirit. The 70 may not be called into a fivefold ministry, but they are focused and can greatly serve under the leadership of a fivefold minister. These are those small group leaders, outreach workers, kingdom financiers, youth workers, musicians, deacons, and the like; who show a higher level of commitment. Their contribution can have a significant impact.

Within this tier of 70, there are elders. But this type of elder is different from a fivefold minister. Instead, they are intermediaries between the congregation and the fivefold ministry. They have the maturity to be informative to the assembly as one under the authority of fivefold ministry while simultaneously being able to assist the visionary leader and other fivefold ministers associated with the visionary leader in spiritual matters pertaining to the world and congregation. They are spiritually mature enough to handle the weightier matters but relatable enough to be more accessible to the congregation. These types of elders are great for leading intercessory prayer and teaching classes on spiritual truths that require a higher level of maturity. For example, Moses needed help judging matters over Israel. He could not be everywhere at once, and the burden became too heavy. He appointed 70 spiritually mature people to help him rule the people. These 70 were not fivefold ministers, but they were elders (Numbers 11:16-25).

Furthermore, one can see this intermediary elder in Acts 15:22: "*Then the apostles [fivefold elders] and elders [intermediary elders], with the whole church [congregational workers of ministry], decided to choose some of their own men and send them to Antioch with Paul and Barnabas*" (brackets mine). Notice the order in this scripture. 1) The apostles were in the representation of the fivefold ministry. 2) Then elders, followed by the 3) congregation. In other words, some elders functioned as a link or liaison between fivefold ministers and the congregation. The other elders mentioned after the apostles could have consisted of fivefold ministers, which is possible! Nonetheless, it does not negate that in scripture, some elders were fivefold ministers, and others were elders in support of the fivefold ministry. Every fivefold minister must be an elder, but only some elders are fivefold ministers.

Interestingly every Christian in this scripture contributed some insight or support in sending people into the mission field with Paul and Barnabas. Each Christian participated in the mission of God. All Christians are supposed to serve on behalf of Christ for His Church and the world.

Governmental/headship ministry: Fivefold ministry (elders) is for those disciples who have so walked with Jesus that they reflect His character (Galatians 2:20). Christ Himself has appointed them. They live sacrificially for the betterment of others. They can teach, guide, love, correct, rebuke, and strengthen the Church as Jesus leads them.

Twelfth tier: At this tier, the disciples have names and faces. Christians, as well as secular people, are aware that Peter, Andrew, James the son of Zebedee, John, Phillip, Bartholomew,

Thomas, Matthew, James the son of Alphaeus, Thaddaeus, Simon the Zealot and Judas; were the original apostles, Jesus had chosen. At this tier, these are the believers selected for Christian governmental leadership over others (Luke 6:13).

Third tier: This is a place of revelation. Out of all the other disciples, Peter, James, and John had a unique relationship with Christ apart from the other disciples. Christ did not love them more. It simply implies that they had different roles and responsibilities within the 12 disciples. Nonetheless, there were moments in Christ's ministry where He only wanted to display His glory and power to them at the exclusion of the others.

Peter, James, and John were the only disciples present when Jesus was transfigured and Moses and Elijah appeared (Matthew 17:1); when Jesus healed Jairus' daughter (Mark 5:37), and when Jesus was in the Garden of Gethsemane (Mark 14:33). All three events were significant. And three specific disciples were chosen to be present. These leaders walked in a greater spiritual revelation and authority than the other disciples. As such, whenever one hears them teach, preach, or operate, there tends to be a sense of the "more than." At this tier, what they say and do is genuinely and succinctly revealed to them by the glory of God—it is not just human wisdom or good thoughts, but it comes from a deeply rooted encounter with God, so much so that people can glean and receive from their experience. Similar to how Jesus' contemporaries responded to Him, modern listeners react to the leaders of this tier in the same manner: "*The people were all so amazed that they asked each other, 'What is this? A new teaching—and with authority! He even gives orders to impure spirits and they obey him'*" (Mark 1:27).

First tier: Here is not only a place of revelation but GREAT revelation of God's glory and power! Moreover, it is a deeper level of intimacy with Christ. If there is one disciple's/apostle's relationship with Christ that I deeply admire, it would be John's. It seems that John had the greatest admiration for Jesus and was the closest to Him.

John was the only disciple to rest his head on Jesus' chest at the dinner table (John 13:23). When all the other disciples disappeared, John was right there at the foot of the cross, watching His Savior die! Jesus thought so much of John that He asked him to care for His mother before He died (John 19:25-27). John would consistently be lingering around the presence of Jesus (John 21:20). He had such access to God that the Lord gave him a revelation that still confounds us to this day (the book of Revelation).

This type of minister has access to God's mysteries; in fact, they have become a mystery or a spectacle to those that meet them. These ministers are like Enoch and Elijah, who were so close to God that they did not taste death. Few ministers have so put away the works of the flesh that the glory of God rests on them. At this level, God is the only subject that matters. And one knows that God uniquely is upon these leaders after being in their presence.

There is enough space for three disciples (Peter, James, and John) on the Mountain of Transfiguration, but there was only space for one when John received his revelation on the island of Patmos. Many Israelites had experienced the presence and power of God, but only Moses had the glory of God shining on his face (Exodus 34:29-35). This type of minister is sold out to the presence of God! Do not expect them to do the traditional workings of a pastor. But rest assured that once they get out of the presence of God, they will reveal truth to the body of Christ that is transformative. All Christians have access to Christ, but these ministers have so left the world behind, and nothing is hindering them from the presence of Jesus.

POSITIONAL KNOWLEDGE

For God's kingdom to progress on earth, Christians have to know their place as a minister. Not all of us will be governmental ministers. Just imagine, for a moment, a church where everyone is an apostle! Apostles are great leaders. As a result, we could never get anything done as the body of Christ because if all were apostles, then everyone would want to be in charge. It would be a chaotic experience as all these apostles were jockeying to have a prominent place of leadership within a church as people were trying to figure out which one indeed was appointed by God. If this type of chaos sounds familiar, it is because this is a frequent problem in churches.

Many people seem to believe they have the same authority as any fivefold minister, especially the pastor or visionary leader of a local church. But as stated previously, the visionary leader has information or access to God in a way a congregational member does not. Just because we all have access to Jesus does not mean He gives us all the same degree of information concerning what must be done.

Remember, God told Moses to tell the Israelites to only take enough manna for the day. God tested the Israelites to see if they would follow His instructions (Exodus 16:4). Notice that God's instruction came through Moses! It did not come through any other Israelite. The scripture says, "*Then Moses said to them, 'No one is to keep any of it until morning.' However, some of them paid no attention to Moses; they kept part of it until morning, but it was full of maggots and began to smell. So Moses was angry with them*" (Exodus 16:19-20). As was always the case, Moses had information the rest of the Israelites did not. The Israelites received Moses' command as a suggestion, but Moses knew God wanted to test their obedience. Sometimes we think we are saying "no" to the person we see, whereas we are actually saying "no" to God. God was fully supporting

Moses as His messenger, but the people refused to listen to Moses, effectively not listening to God.

In the book of Acts 5:1-11, a husband and wife attempt to lie to the Apostle Peter in the church offering. They pretended to give all the money they had from selling a property, wherein they were holding some of the funds. They thought they were lying to a man known as Peter. However, Peter tells them they lied to the Holy Spirit, and they both die. And while the Holy Spirit is merciful, this passage should give Christians a cause to pause and consider that how we treat people might be how we are treating the Holy Spirit.

The good news is that God is a God of mercy. He prefers to show us mercy (Hosea 6:6). If you still have breath in your lungs, there is time to get it right. The bottom line is that we all have access to Jesus. However, if you are not the visionary leader of a church house, do not assume you have all the information, and never allow the Devil to trick you into believing your church leader is against you! There are false church leaders. But there are a lot of good ones that genuinely have access to information that will advance your life.

LIMITED CAPACITY

What is your capacity? Have you ever earnestly inquired of the Lord concerning your role? If God told you to be the church janitor, landscape worker, media specialist, greeter, Sunday school teacher, small group leader, intercessor, or armor bearer in support of the pastor, would you do it? If God asked you to be a parking lot attendant, to place pens and offering envelopes in the seats, and prepare coffee and snacks at every church meeting, could you do it? Or are you only willing to do what is comfortable for you?

The ministry call of God on a person's life will never be comfortable. Sometimes people want ministry positions beyond their capacity because they want to feel prestigious. For some people, no matter how much they want to be a pastor, that is not where God has called them. Should they supersede God's plan for their lives and attempt to be a pastor/visionary leader of a church house, they will be a distraction by recruiting undiscerning Christians that should not be under their false leadership.

When Moses needed elders to help support him in his ministry, he chose officials and put them over a certain number of people: "*He chose capable men from all Israel and made them leaders of the people, officials over thousands, hundreds, fifties and tens*" (Exodus 18:25). Each of these "capable men" were only as capable as their capacity, which means that if the leader of "tens" tried to be a leader of "thousands" that would be out of order.

The point is that people can slip out of the will of God because of selfish ambition (Philippians 2:3). They want more or less than what God told them to do. God has called some to be visionary leaders of large and small churches, others to be deacons, and others to be ministry workers (outreach, kitchen ministry, media). If one is in the will of God, then that is where he or she is supposed to be.

For example, some people have been told for their whole life by their mother that they are excellent singers—and of course, a mother may like to hear her children sing. But their voices are inadequate and would not be well received by others. Many people may think they should be on the worship team because of what their parents think, but God has not called them to that ministry.

In some instances, God places an individual in a position for a season and will eventually promote him or her to a different position entirely. (E.g., David would eventually be promoted from Saul's armor bearer to the King.) But, there are people whose current ministry does not lead to a positional change, but they are to maximize or multiply what they have. Both instances can be seen in what has become known as The "Parable of the Talents." Jesus tells the story of a master who gives his servants talents: "*To one he gave five bags of gold, to another two bags, and to another one bag, each according to **his ability**. Then he went on his journey*" (Matthew 25:15, emphasis mine). Consider that the master only gave to their "ability," meaning they only had enough gold to support their skillset.

Some lawyers make exceptionally more money, given their ability, while others make less, given their capacity. But if some lawyers are willing to maximize or even multiply their ability, they could make more money. Likewise, the characters in this parable were given according to their ability. But two of the three servants invested and multiplied the gold they were given, while the other simply maintained the status quo. Two ways to interpret the position of the servants:

1) The position was not to change for these servants; they were still servants regardless of how much gold each received. Nonetheless, they all were to increase in the position they were placed. Some people are deacons, worship leaders, and workers of various ministers, and their status will never change because God requires them to be where they are.

2) The position they were in would eventually change if they had passed the test of managing the master's gold correctly. When the master congratulates the faithful servant(s), he says, "*Well done, good and faithful servant! You have been faithful with a few things; I will put you in charge of many things*" (23). Perhaps being in "charge of many things" was a positional change?

Regardless of whatever interpretation one chooses, the faithful servants' happiness significantly increased because of their obedience. The master says, "*Come and share your master's happiness*" (Matthew 25:23).

In 2 Chronicles chapter 2, King Solomon began to build the temple for the Lord. Here, Solomon hires thousands upon thousands of people to make the temple. Thousands of supervisors, stone cutters, yarn workers, lumberjacks, and grunt workers to carry the material. With all these positions needed to build the temple for the Lord, Solomon says, "'*The temple I am going to build will be great, because our God is greater than all other gods...*" (2 Chronicles 2:5).

As Solomon said, I say to you that what you do for God is "great." You need to see it the way God does! Not everyone gets to be King Solomon (visionary leader)—God has designated leaders to keep things in order. And if everyone truly understood the pressure to be in that position, there would be less desire for it. Nevertheless, you play a significant role in building or advancing God's kingdom. Do you think God despised the work of any of these people? Or was He overjoyed to see so many people play a role in building the temple? You know the answer! Realize your capacity, fulfill your part, and God will be pleased.

CHAPTER FOUR

SETTING THE CULTURE PART ONE

U nderstanding that the visionary leader must establish the kingdom culture for any given church is essential. Without question, every church should attempt to bring glory to God through Jesus Christ and be concerned with His kingdom—if Jesus is not exclusively the focal point, then it is not a church. So there will be similarities between churches concerning salvific doctrine and general understandings of faith and conduct. For example, one of the most explicit understandings of Christian culture is found in "The Sermon on the Mount" in the book of Matthew. From chapters 5-7, Jesus lays out what it means to be one of His followers and a citizen of His kingdom. Historically, and even today, Christians receive "The Sermon on the Mount" as one of the central teachings of the Christian faith.

While the principles and the objectives of glorifying God remain the same, how matters of faith and conduct are expressed may look different from church to church, but they should never contradict the written scripture. Why? Because each visionary leader is different.

Both Samuel and Elijah were men of God. They are great prophets. But they are different because Samuel seems a little more relaxed and regal. In contrast, Elijah comes across as fiery and frantic. Samuel comes across as more diplomatic and willing to have governmental discourse, while Elijah is more confrontational and displays God's power. Samuel and Elijah had followers. So given the difference in style or methodology, can you imagine how different each of their students would be?

Possibly the type of students Samuel attracted were more studious and proper. And perhaps the students of Elijah were bold and brazen. No doubt Elijah's most remarkable student, Elisha, was brash like his predecessor.

The main objective always remains the same! God desires to redeem humanity through His Son, Jesus Christ. God fills His people with His Holy Spirit so they may live like Jesus on this earth. And if one makes much of the grace given, that person will pursue and experience God's kingdom on this earth and when Christ returns! Hallelujah! Each church will carry the essentials of faith and conduct while having a unique mission or way of expressing love to the Creator. The church of Corinth is different from the church of Thessalonica. The church at Corinth was primarily focused on spiritual gifts and the works of the Holy Spirit (Pneumatology). In contrast, the church at Thessalonica was more concerned with the afterlife or what happened when someone died (Eschatology).

Some churches emphasize music as the conduit to bring glory to God, while others have a studious approach and provide a lot of Bible studies. Some churches are more evangelistic and outreach driven. Others are motivated to intercessory prayer and sustain regular and long prayer meetings for their communities. There is a choir in some churches, while others have a worship band. Some are casual in attire, while others are formal. The leader will determine the style of said church.

In the following sections, I will address what I believe to be the most crucial cultural subject in every church—worship. I cannot cover everything in this one chapter, nor should I pretend my experience is universal. Nonetheless, the next section is a part of what I teach leaders and Christian workers in my ministry, and hopefully, it helps you to be a faithful minister or congregational member.

WORSHIP STYLE

David was a musician and dancer. David would play his harp when demons tormented his mentor King Saul. This would ease the suffering of Saul (1 Samuel 16:23). Furthermore, as the Ark of the Covenant (God's presence) was entering David's city, scripture says that David began to dance with all his "might." As David celebrated, so did the people. They were shouting and blowing trumpets. In other words, if you wanted to know how to respond to the presence of God, it was David, the visionary leader, who was the model (2 Samuel 6:14-15).

Often when people think of a "worship leader" or "worship pastor," they think of someone with a musical ability who is leading a band or choir at a worship gathering. But worship is more than just musicality. Indeed every aspect of a church is worship: The preaching of God's word, how Christians treat one another, the offering, and other things all equate to a form of worship to God. Therefore, while everyone participates and there are those designated to lead parts of worship, the prominent worship leader is the visionary leader.

If one has a charismatic leader, who likes to shout and dance in the presence of God, then that is the appropriate worship style at that particular church. Some leaders are more quiet and reflective in worship, and the congregation responds similarly. In some settings, people play the tambourine, wave flags, lift hands, lay prostrate on the floor, close their eyes, and more. So long as it is not sinful, God receives the worship of someone with a genuine heart toward Him.

NO DISTRACTIONS

One of the most disheartening things for a true visionary leader is seeing the apathy of the people he is leading. The visionary leader sees it all. He will notice when people are on their phones during the worship service, when they are talking about other things during the preaching, and how they leave quickly and do not want to engage with God's people. Even when the preaching and music are powerfully anointed, some will still be found sleeping or disinterested while claiming they love Christ. It was no different in Jesus' time.

There would be pharisees or religious leaders surrounding Jesus as He confounded and captivated crowds with preaching, signs, wonders, and miracles—but they remained uninspired. Jesus asked His disciples to watch and pray for one hour while He was in agony, and every time He went to check on them, they were sleeping (Matthew 26:40). And Jesus expressed His dissatisfaction with the fact that they kept sleeping on Him. There can be dry worship services with non-anointed men and women leading. And sometimes, leaders have rough days. But all of God's people are to actively engage in worship. At Jesus' birth, wise men came to present their gifts to Jesus. They came with worship/gifts for the newborn King. They were not expecting someone else to compensate for their lack of worship or to motivate them.

Is God not enough to captivate us? Like the children of Israel in the wilderness, have we become apathetic in our thanksgiving to God? Are we no longer impressed with the Red Sea being parted? Are we not satisfied when manna rains from heaven? Have we become calloused in our response to our salvation? God saved us! Such a thought is worthy of our full attention when we gather for worship!

Notice the level of intentionality and focus when Moses worshiped God:

Now Moses used to take a tent and pitch it outside the camp some distance away, calling it the "tent of meeting." Anyone inquiring about the Lord would go to the tent of meeting

outside the camp. And whenever Moses went out to the tent,
all the people rose and stood at the entrances to their tents,
watching Moses until he entered the tent. As Moses went
into the tent, the pillar of cloud would come down and stay
at the entrance, while the Lord spoke with Moses. (Exodus.
33:7-9, emphasis mine)

When God's presence appeared in this tent, everyone
worshiped! There were no distractions. Not only did Moses
worship, but they all did. How could anyone be so
unresponsive, critical, and distracted when God's presence is
among us?

There should be no unnecessary talking or distractions
during a worship service. The exception is when one has to give
an individual instruction to a child or adult. (E.g., a person
informs the person sitting next to him or her that they have to
leave early.) Perhaps it is a lively service where the preacher
expects people to talk back to him during the service in regard
to the message. (E.g., "Amen," and "Hallelujah," among other
phrases or commentary that are appropriate.) Church members
should not intentionally distract other members during the
music, preaching, scripture reading, and altar calls. And even
between the transitions of movement in service, God's people
should keep a heart of praise. Here are three things that happen
as a result of a distracted congregation:

Sabotages the visionary leader: When people talk while the
visionary leader is preaching or addressing the congregation
regarding the church, they are teaching the people around them
that what the leader says is unimportant. They are
unconsciously sabotaging the leader's authority. As if to say,
"He may be the leader, but what I or we have to say is more
important." God chose the leader to be His representative.

Hence, what the leader says under the inspiration of the Holy Spirit is always of consequence.

Sabotages someone's ability to receive: God could be trying to heal or give someone an answer to a prayer, but if the person is distracted by other thoughts or people, he or she might miss God. Just imagine the preacher saying something that is a direct answer for many. But the intended recipients miss it because another person in the congregation is trying to show them something funny on his or her phone! What was said could have radically changed their perspective on their spouse or job, but they go back to the same broken situation without the needed answer because of the distraction.

Sabotages God: Ultimately, this is all about God. It is distasteful and insulting to God when one does not give Him undivided attention in a worship gathering. The funny video on a phone, the nap, jokes, and thoughts surrounding what one will eat or do midweek can all wait until after the service. The Lord sees the heart. And He does not have to accept tainted worship. Please, between the time the worship service starts and ends, give God your attention. He is so worthy of our praise. Do not grieve the Holy Spirit (Ephesians 4:30).

We must also have the flexibility for people who come to our worship services with mental handicaps or social disorders. An autistic person may not understand all the social cues of when not or when to speak. Someone with ADHD may struggle with focus. However, people with disabilities should be welcomed to our worship services. And each visionary leader must keep in mind the various needs of those he is ministering to. Nonetheless, there should be a reverence for God in each service.

TRUE WORSHIP

I believe the bases for all Christian worship should begin with this question: "What does God desire?" If we start with that question, we will not design our worship services to attract people but God. Without a doubt, we do want churches filled with people worshiping God. Jesus did die for a community. Nonetheless, if people do not show up, that is not the worst of our problems, as God would still be worshiped without people. Scripture makes it clear that angels and all of creation worship God (Isaiah 6:1-3, Psalm 19:1). So our most serious inquiry should be to affirm whether God attends our worship services because there is a type of worship God wants.

Jesus spoke to a Samaritan woman at a well. She was a woman with a questionable lifestyle. Moreover, the fact that Jewish people and Samaritans had a racial conflict with each other caused her to resist Jesus at first. She argued about the proper place of worship. To her surprise, Jesus points her to a better way. In essence, He explains to her that worship has nothing to do with a physical location or race but has everything to do with the Spirit and truth. Jesus claims that God is seeking that kind of worship from people (John 4:7-26)!

Jesus did not make the issue about contemporary versus traditional music; He did not use racial descriptives such as a "black church" or "white church." He did not concern Himself with the economic and social status of those that would worship. He was not even worried about a physical building. What Jesus claimed He wanted most, what He claimed God was looking for, is genuine worship devoid of falsehoods, gimmicks, posing, and manipulation; worship full of truth and His Spirit.

King David had the type of worship God desired. As the majority celebrated with David as the Ark came into the city, not everyone did! Michal, David's wife, looked from afar with disgust at the worship of her husband. Her father was the king before David. So I imagine she had a reference point for how kings should worship. If it was not like her father, it was wrong. Hence, when David returned home, she attempted to insult him, but he reminded Michal that God chose him over her father. Why did God choose him? Because all David wanted to do was be pleasing to his God. As David danced, he was not thinking about his position as king or how pleasant he appeared to everyone around him. He just wanted God.

God is looking for verifiable and bonafide worship from those that love Him. He does not need it, but He does welcome it. God enjoys His creation and invites us to enjoy Him. Worship is not about our personal preference. It is a shame that some people choose churches based on the style of music, preaching, clothing, building, skin color, and location. Some have spoken against churches as if they were sinful because of their style. And we ought to be careful! Even if it is not our preference, it could be God's! Worship is about Him (2 Samuel 6:16-22).

The sad reality is that after Michal criticizes David for his worship of God, the passage ends by saying Michal was barren for the rest of her life (23). She did not produce children. In other words, she had no legacy because she despised true worship. May your life not be barren! May you choose to worship in Spirit and truth as David did. May the legacy you leave behind be one of true worship to God. When worship truly becomes about God, His presence shows up, people are physically healed, answers are received, and salvation takes place. As God is looking for true worshipers, may you be found by Him!

CHAPTER FIVE

SETTING THE CULTURE PART TWO

Consider how in the last chapter, we gained an understanding of worship and its importance in that worship is foundational to all the Christian does. Christians understand that worship is essential to their practice. In other words, if our kingdom culture is to worship or honor God, then everything we do in the Church should reflect that aim.

When the posture of one's heart and mind has become consumed with the self, all of one's endeavors concerning church protocol lead to glorifying oneself or self-preservation. As a result of self-absorption, a church's organizational structure and exploits are limited to one's "traditions." In contrast, God may want to do something new in the community or within a church. But due to carnal concerns or being too uncomfortable, some churches refuse to adapt. This was the problem of the pharisees. They relied on their traditions that upheld their social status instead of embracing Christ's way. For the sake of clarity, the word of God does not change. God's biblical principles and character will remain regardless of what period or how the secular culture changes. However, methodologies, styles, and people will change.

For example, I love the old hymns—there is a rich history and beautiful theology attached to them. Nonetheless, styles change. A church's worship of God is not qualified or disqualified by whether they worship with a hymnal. Some say that hymnals are too antiquated and boring. Others criticize that contemporary worship music is too repetitive and lacks theological depth. Yet, in the Bible, the angels that worship around God's throne had great theology and were repetitive in their worship (Isaiah 6:3). What if God likes both theology and, at times, words repeated in our worship? Even if no one else thinks it, my wife and children never get tired of me telling them how beautiful they are. Perhaps what some receive as repetitive and boring, God receives as pleasant!

Worship in all its aspects (musically, financially, janitorial, preaching) is about God's preference, not our own. And it just so happens that what matters to God most is the inward posture towards Him in worship (Psalm 51:17). There is nothing inherently evil about a church meeting in a lovely ornate building, but how that church uses the building could be. There is nothing inherently wrong about Christian hip hop or rap—it is just a type of melody, but what is said about God in the lyrics could be. In other words, sometimes, what we think is ungodly is just something we do not prefer.

This chapter will attempt to place God's preference over your own regarding the style or methodology of a given church. I understand that each church has a different mission for each context. So while the following subheadings will not be all-inclusive, they should highlight many kingdom aspects God expects of His churches.

FAMILY

One of the overwhelming concepts of the Christian faith is family. We know that family is essential since God established it in the garden. One understands that values differ from one family to another regarding earthly family. Even though God's family is diverse in its preference towards music, clothing, and recreational styles, specific values must be maintained throughout all Christian denominations, associations, and

fellowships—God loves His people. He expects His children to get along with
one another. In scripture, God abundantly clarifies that He and His children are a package. You cannot accept one without the other (1 John 4:20).

Family is so foundational to the Christian experience that believers are told to prefer Christian brothers and sisters more than those outside of the Church (Galatians 6:10). This does not mean that we are not to demonstrate love and mercy to unbelievers. It means we should significantly show those virtues to one another even more.

On one occasion, while Jesus was ministering, He was informed that His mother and brothers were looking for Him. He used the brief interruption as an opportunity to teach, and claimed that His family were those that did His Father's will (Matthew 12:46-50). Essentially, He was not going to stop ministering to other people to wait on His natural family at this moment. It was more important to do the will of His Father. And while Jesus loved His biological family, He wanted His followers to understand that being a part of God's family is more important. The people at church are important to God. They are your family. God watches how we treat one another.

ARMY

Another overwhelming aspect of the Church is the idea of being in the Lord's army. And while many believers have heard this before, I do not believe many Christians have truly conceptualized it as they did in the early church. The early church had a sense that they were in a real war! The Bible talks about Christians having weapons, armor, fighting, and advancing. But there has been a sabotaging of these thoughts, which is evident in some of the phrases Christians use:

"We are all the same": This is true in that before Christ entered a person's life, one was a sinner who needed to be saved. But just like in any good army, there is such a thing as rank! What has been seen throughout scripture is that God places people in leadership positions to lead His people.

I have five children. They are equal because they are my children, whom I love equally. But they are not equal in terms of talents, gifts, and maturity. Typically speaking, whenever parents leave the house, they put the most mature child in charge. The other kids might be more talented in other areas compared to the oldest child, but the eldest child is left in charge because of his or her stronger decision-making skills. Likewise, the obvious example of this would be the visionary leader of a church house.

Periodically God's children compete against one another instead of embracing their role to advance God's Kingdom. Church members who are not qualified, authorized, or called will try to outdo their pastor, deacons, and other people in ministry positions (Acts 15:24). There is plenty of ministry for everybody. However, the narrative of Cain and Able tends to play itself repeatedly in modern Christianity. And while it is not always physical blood that is spilled, sometimes Christians try to kill a brother's or sister's influence or impact when they are jealous. We cannot lose the war; Christ has secured that for us, but we sure do lose many battles because Christians step out of order.

"I get a lot out of it": The Church is where one can receive. God is a good God who blesses His children. And yet, in an army, one is called to make a real sacrifice. The early church was willing to make financial sacrifices and even give up their lives for the advancement of God's kingdom. They sold their homes and shared among other believers (Acts 2:44-45). They knew God would reward them for their sacrifice in this life and the next. But their motivation was to be pleasing to God (2 Timothy 2:4).

Sadly, sometimes in the modern church, people believe that God's will is only to bless them with monetary or physical gain. Let us not forget that even the Devil wants to bless you with such things as long as it distracts you from the mission of God. One will receive good things from God, but Christians should not forget that they are enlisted in the Lord's army. And in an army, Christians give sacrificially for the advancement of our King. The Apostle Paul went through many trials in his service to the Lord. And yet, towards the end of his life, he was pleased to have sacrificed for the Lord. In fact, like a good soldier, Paul desired to live sacrificially like Christ (Philippians 3:10). Not all of us are called to live a life like Paul. And we can enjoy luxuries in life. However, it cannot always be about "getting" but rather "giving." Even Christ taught us that one is more blessed when they give than when they receive (Acts 20:35).

"My season is up": The Lord's army is the only army where deserters are seen as noble. People quickly leave once offended, misunderstand, or do not get what they want. The hypocrisy in the church is not that we make mistakes and, at times, bad choices—Christ's sacrifice on the cross makes up for those circumstances. But instead, many only stay committed when they "feel" like it. Will God sometimes call you to participate in a ministry or church for a season? Absolutely! Nonetheless, many Christians quit too early because they are emotionally unstable, do not want to submit to leadership, and do not want to be challenged, corrected, or changed in any way.

When Jesus multiplied the fish and the loaves, a great crowd of 5,000 began to follow Him. When He tells that same crowd hard theology, the overwhelming majority walk away from Him. Because Jesus made them uncomfortable, they left him (John 6:25-66). The same is true today! Many people only follow Christ so long as there is no difficulty. But Jesus never promised His people life without difficulty. He said the contrary: "*In this world, you will have trouble. But take heart! I have overcome the world*" (John 16:33b).

Christians give up too early. Just like in Bible times, modern Christians choose to die in the wilderness instead of possessing the land; they prefer the company and pleasure of Delilah instead of committing to their calling; they fall asleep instead of staying awake for one hour to pray with Jesus (Matthew 26:40)! Thank God for grace; we all need it. Nonetheless, our faith needs to be stronger than our feelings. We leave churches too soon when God might be asking us to bunker down like good soldiers.

"The church is a hospital": Jesus did relate His ministry to that of a doctor (Matthew 9:12). Jesus was unlike any other doctor the world has ever seen. A woman had a blood issue for twelve years, and physicians could not heal her. She decided to locate Jesus. Upon finding Him, she believed that if she touched the hem of His garment, she would be healed, and she was (Mark 5:23-34). Jesus could do what doctors could not do.

Because Jesus heals, His Church is a place for healing. People can be healed physically, mentally, and spiritually. Furthermore, everyone Jesus healed was able to return to society. So while the Church, in many ways, is likened to a hospital, one should get better! One does not stay chronically broken! In addition, military bases have hospitals where soldiers recover and get back into the war, or some are discharged because their injuries are too significant. But because Jesus never did an incomplete healing, God's people should always fully recover and get back in the fight.

Even if one has to endure hardships like Job, be physically beaten like the apostles, and go through the many trials like the writer of Hebrews highlights (read Hebrews 11:32-40), the ailments are only there to show how victorious the believer is despite circumstance and to bring glory to God. The three Hebrew boys counted it a privilege and honor to be thrown into the fiery furnace for God. They knew that God could save them, but they believed that if God saw fit for them to die in the furnace, they welcomed being a martyr for the glory of God (Daniel 3:18).

Notice what Paul says about his hardships: "*Therefore we do not lose heart. Though outwardly we are wasting away, yet inwardly we are being renewed day by day. For our light and momentary troubles are achieving for us an eternal glory that far outweighs them all. So we fix our eyes not on what is seen, but on what is unseen, since what is seen is temporary, but what is unseen is eternal*" (2 Corinthians 4:16-18). At times, the people of God endure some type of affliction. And yet, the believer is always "renewed" and radiant. What confounds the world is how victorious and whole the Christian is despite suffering. There is a joy we have the world cannot understand (Philippians 4:4-6).

If the church is just a hospital, its members are nothing more than patients. Christians should not stay chronically ill or broken. No doubt, there are times when one is harmed and needs time to recover. But one does recover and continue. Even if God does allow someone to walk with a limp like Jacob, it will be for the glory of God! Otherwise, the church becomes a place whose culture is self-pity, pain, irritation, and discomfort. The preaching becomes watered down and medicinal—like getting a morphine shot to dull or numb the pain without the promise of ever being whole. Church becomes like hospice where one is just waiting for death. Church becomes like the lame man with a victimhood mentality as he complains that no one helped him into the healing pool (John 5:1-11).

When Christians stay hurt, they cannot become what God intended them to be! Furthermore, why would anyone desire to be a Christian if the result is being reduced to a figurative/ spiritual hospital bed? No, Christ is a healer! Presently, He still does signs, wonders, and miracles. As He was willing to cure the leper (Matthew 8:2-3), He is ready to heal the believer. The Christian is called to soldier on.

GOD'S HOUSE

What matters the most is God's will for His Church. The mission can differ for each church house, but the purpose cannot change—to glorify God. For one church, God's mission is to focus on the inner city; for another, it is to launch missionaries overseas; for another, to produce a ministry that reaches out to the marketplace. Whatever the mission, God's glory should be the chief aim.

Over and over again, the scripture reminds us that God is after His glory. He does things for His namesake; He makes oaths on His name because no other name has such integrity (Hebrews 6:13-15); His name is above all other names. This thought resides in scripture but should also be magnified in the Church.

For instance, Jesus was angry with a temple/church because it became commercialized and stole money. He said, "'*My house will be called a house of prayer,' but you are making it a den of robbers*'" (Matthew 21:13). The people were not only stealing money but also stealing God's praise—it became about human gain, instead of divine connection with God. Hence, a saying goes like this: "My house, my rules." The Church is God's house, and He is the one that rules. May the Christian abandon selfish ambition and pursue God's will. The Christian should always ask: "Do I only worship God when I get what I prefer, or do I worship for His glory?"

CHAPTER SIX

SETTING THE CULTURE PART THREE

The Bible teaches that children are likened to inheritance and reward (Psalm 127:3). While some people do not want children, many believe that part of their legacy includes children. They want to pass on their knowledge, passions, faith, and so on. As a father, I enjoy seeing my physical likeness in my children.

There are times when my children behave like me. There is a natural and supernatural bond between parent and child. And one thing parents do not like seeing is their children fighting—neither does God want to see His children fighting.

Scripture makes it clear that those who have received salvation have been adopted into God's family (Romans 8:15). We are children of God and even joint heirs with Christ (Romans 8:17). Children are a reminder of their predecessors. When people see the faith and conduct of God's children, it is the reminder or testimony that Christ did walk this earth, and He is coming again. Even when Peter tried to deny Jesus, he could not hide it, for people said his speech sounded like he had been with Christ (Matthew 26:73).

The Christian sounds and behaves like Christ. God's people do make mistakes, but the scripture encourages us to become like Him: "*Therefore, as God's chosen people, holy and dearly loved, clothe yourselves with compassion, kindness, humility, gentleness, and patience*" (Colossians 3:12). In other words, as God's children we should be embracing and treating each other well in the church. It should be delightful and pleasing when

Christians gather together (Psalm 133:1). One needs to ask themselves: "What is hindering me from loving my brothers and sisters?" Hopefully, with the following subheadings, one will understand how important interpersonal relationships are within the church.

CHURCH ATTENDANCE

The typical Christian does not always conceptualize the importance of church attendance. Because what one thinks about the Church is what one thinks about Christ. Scripture makes it very clear that the Church is the physical and spiritual representation of Christ (1 Corinthians 12:12-27). Jesus is the head of the Church. Hence, when Christians claim to not need a local church body, their decision reflects more on their relationship with Christ than the people that attend.

Some say they do not attend church because they do not like "organized religion." But what is the alternative? Perhaps "chaos religion?" I understand the gist of such statements in that Jesus is more than just rules and a physical building. I do accept that people have been abused in certain church settings. No doubt there have been sex scandals concerning children and adults at church, money laundering, and manipulation on large scales. Yet, what immature or false converts do does not change how glorious God intended His Church to be.

Jesus made it very clear that within His church, there would always be true and false converts (Matthew 13:24-30). Even Jesus had a false convert in His group (Judas). In other words, hurt feelings are not a sufficient enough reason to stay away from a local church. Jesus was hurt and ultimately rejected by His people, and He still thought they were worth Him being sacrificed. It is by no stretch of the imagination to say: "Christ thought you were worth dying for!" And now He regularly prays for us while seated next to the Father (Romans 8:34).

If Jesus sat and ate with sinners, believers can learn to be obedient and fellowship with other Christians—even the "hard to love" ones. The apostles regularly met at the temple (church) (Acts 2:46). They continued to meet with the rebellious religious order that criticized their Lord. Jesus' attendance was regular at the synagogues and temple (Luke 4:16, John 8:2). We are encouraged and commanded in the book of Hebrews to gather as believers regularly (Hebrews 10:25).

It is a mistake to think that Jesus wanted to revolutionize the Church. As if to throw away all that was done before. No, on the contrary, He came to reform (I.g., embrace the good parts while exposing and eradicating the harmful elements) the Church. There were many good things about Judaism; yet, it missed the true heart of worship. Jesus will not throw away the importance of His church due to hurt feelings. Does God care when His children have been abused? Indeed, He does. Does He revenge the wrongdoings that have happened to His children? He does (Romans 12:19)! God may call one to another church when abuse has occurred. But He no less calls us to gather.

Any parent loves to see their children meeting together. Parents rejoice to see their adult children return home during special celebrations or holidays. Parents love when their adult children continue to have a relationship with one another. Siblings have no choice but to live in the same household as children. Hence, it is beautiful and nostalgic to see one's children continue in their sibling relationships as adults. It is a unique feeling of accomplishment for parents. So let us not nullify what Christ did for us. He died for a family that would continue to gather. Despite all resistance, the following statement I make needs to be said: It is disobedience to not belong to a church. God will lead an individual to a local body of believers.

RECONCILIATION

While I want to be sensitive to extreme acts of abuse that have happened in some churches, it needs to be stated that one should not be shocked when their feelings are hurt in the church. Many Christians have left good churches because of how they felt or what they assumed. They had not grown in their maturity to understand that there is tension and harmful things get said within every family.

Siblings fight! It has always been that way. If one grew up in a household with more than one child, there was controversy, conflict, and confusion. Siblings fought over the restroom, the TV remote, the attention of the parents, and many things. In the Bible, some siblings do not get along well. Cain kills Able, Joseph is thrown into a pit by his brothers, David's older brother rejects him, Martha thinks Mary is lazy, and the disciples bicker among themselves. There will be fighting or disagreements among members of the same church, but we are supposed to fight well. Christians must stop thinking there must be something morally wrong when they disagree with other believers. Sometimes there are misunderstandings that can be clarified through confrontative yet, loving interaction.

Scripture teaches that Christians have been given the vocation of reconciliation. Jesus does not even accept our worshipful acts if we have unresolved conflicts with other Christians. Christ told us to reconcile to our Christian brother or sister first, and then He would accept our worship (Matthew 5:24). One is not a mature Christian if he or she prefers division over reconciliation.

Sometimes mediation is necessary when there is a conflict between believers (Matthew 18). There is such a thing as an authority in God's house. And at times, excommunication is necessary for the harmony of a local church body. Nonetheless, the Bible teaches that love compels us to take care of one another (1 Corinthians 4:8-12).

Unfortunately, there are many Christians who divide over insignificant matters. Sometimes it is one's unresolved inner turmoil that gets projected onto others, which causes one to assume the worse and terminate relationships that were helpful and healthy. And yet, the scriptures inform that healing happens when Christians confide in one another (James 5:16). Of course, the Devil gets involved in church drama. But perhaps the backstabbing and betrayal in a church are due to our lack of trust in one another. Maybe one has not healed from the wounds of the past and, therefore, places unrealistic expectations on fellow believers. "God, give us the courage to confess our sins, heal and pursue reconciliation with one another. Let us follow your example for reconciliation on the cross. Amen!"

MANNERS

While doctrine, signs, wonders, miracles, evangelism, preaching, and helping the needy are paramount to the Christian experience, there are subjects Christians can easily ignore because it does not appear grandiose. Such is the case with good manners. Simply put, God's people should be mannerly. The Apostle Paul claimed that people could be highly gifted and understand mysteries that others do not, but they are nothing without love (1 Corinthians 13:1-3).

In all its aspects, Christian service is robbed of its power when Christians do not display manners. Sometimes when a person has a solid spiritual gift or service, that person mistakenly forgets to show courtesy and respect to others. In his or her subconscious thinking, it is as if this person is saying, "As long as the result is great, people will be happy even if I'm pushy and inconsiderate."

When Christians practice their spiritual gifts or service without manners, people receive from us but reject our God. The secular world thinks: "Why become Christian if it makes you rude... I'll just receive their services."

Unlike popular opinion, maturity is not found in charismatic gifts, Christian service, or how much knowledge one has. Pharaoh's magicians could do supernatural wonders but did not know God; Martha loved to serve, but her service made her competitive and worried about many things; Saul of Tarsus was very knowledgeable, but his knowledge caused him to persecute Christians. This is all to say that Christlike action does not equate to a Christlike character. Following is a list of what has kept many from demonstrating proper Christlike behavior among Christians and secular people:

Do-ology: Scripture teaches that there must be action attached to our faith. However, when actions are devoid of or outweigh intimacy, the relationship is contractual instead of covenantal. Hiring a contractor to fix your roof does not require an intimate relationship with the said contractor. You hire them for a particular skill. But covenantal relationships, such as the biblical understanding of marriage, requires intimacy and a sharing in one's nature. God was covenantal in His relationship with us. He invites us to share in His image, and He even became like His creation (John 1:14).

A Christian can preach to a congregation, serve the community, operate prophetically, and so forth, yet not have a deep relationship with God (Matthew 7:21-23). There are even good moral atheists that serve communities. People cannot pour out what they have not received for themselves. Hence, if our relationship with God is lacking, our relationship with one another will also be.

Me-ology: God does care about His people individually. Yet, what God does for the "me" is always intended for the "we." God always has a great community in mind. Why did God bless Abraham? So that he could be a blessing to others (Genesis 12:2). Why did God make David King? Because He knew all of Israel would be blessed with him on the throne, and Jesus came through the line of David.

When Christians think that church is all about their comfort, they want sermons, leaders, children's programming, the building, and outreaches all to be tailored to their specifications. They have forgotten it is all about the glory of God. This mentality results in pride. Causing a believer to use others as a stepping stone toward their success. Unfortunately, relationships requiring vulnerability become an inconvenience to this immature believer's selfish ambition. Therefore, when the Christian experience becomes all about the self, the relationships that follow this ideology will always be insubstantial and superficial. Like the disciples in the gospel narratives, Christians will desert and deny knowing each other when it gets difficult.

Foe-ology: Life will always be full of opponents, and while antagonists help define the protagonists of the stories we like, Christians are defined by the greatness of their God. If the Devil has his way, he will have you so focused on your enemies that you miss the goodness of God. Everyone you meet will be a potential enemy! This was the problem of characters like Judas and the pharisees. They saw Jesus as a hindrance to their potential instead of embracing Christ as fulfilling their greatest potential.

When Christians are always looking for the next anti-christ, the next Goliath, the next demon, and falsehoods in the government, they mistakenly turn against their brothers and sisters. In other words, Christians divide over political parties instead of real doctrinal issues of the faith. Yes, some enemies require our attention—but not our absolute and eternal attention —that is reserved for God.

When this "foe-ology" goes unchecked for a while, it promotes gossip, slander, and hatred among believers—this should not be. One should not be divided over matters that are not salvific. Secondary topics apart from salvation, such as the casting out of demons, spiritual gifts, secular government, and the like, should not have our attention more than Christ. The real enemy has always been Satan. And because he is a formidable foe, he gets some of our engagement but not all— for we already know his devastating end. "Lord, You alone are worthy of glory and honor. May our focus be on You!"

CHILDREN MATTER

Regarding our interpersonal relationships at church, it is essential to address the matter of children. I assess that the modern church, mainly in the U.S.A., makes an incorrect evaluation of children. God is pro-children. He encourages us to have childlike faith. Jesus claimed that to enter His kingdom, one must be like a child (Matthew 18:3). Contrastingly, there is an admonishment within the Bible to put childlike things behind you and become mature (1 Corinthians 13:11). Nevertheless, there is a part of our faith that is to remain childlike.

Every so often, in the Christian's attempt to be a serious theologian and worshiper, one views children as an annoyance or hindrance. So people try to keep children out of the main worship service. Or when they are in the worship service, people get concerned that they might be too noisy. Many parents worry about bringing their children into the worship service for fear of being a distraction.

No doubt, children should be corrected by their parents when they become unruly. And at a certain age, children or teenagers have to learn to sit quietly without interrupting. Hence, there are some Christian settings where children do not have the situational awareness or patience to attend (E.g., serious studies, deep intercessory prayer). Nevertheless, worship services, particularly the main service when the whole body gathers as one, should be welcoming of children. Even the disciples made the mistake of keeping children from Jesus: *"Then people brought little children to Jesus for him to place his hands on them and pray for them. But the disciples rebuked them. Jesus said, 'Let the little children come to me, and do not hinder them, for the kingdom of heaven belongs to such as these.' When he had placed his hands on them, he went on from there"* (Matthew 19:13-15).

When a church's view of children is that of a hindrance, they tend to conduct themselves in one or more of the following ways:

Lack of discipleship: Children get placed into youth groups or Sunday school classes where they receive more fruit juice and snacks than the Word of God. The teachers or leaders of the group give a quick cursory overview of scripture without much thought put into it. In other words, discipling of children can appear more like babysitting than a genuine attempt to teach who God is and one's response to Him. Of course, there is nothing wrong with having a good time with games and snacks —they are children. And we cannot expect them to be scholars.

Moreover, there needs to be a sufficient amount of workers for the children's ministry. If the same person is doing youth ministry at every worship meeting and never gets the opportunity to worship in the main service, then that person may experience burnout. Yet, due to the person's dedication to the Lord, this individual continues to do youth ministry without the creativity, energy, and depth required to lead the children because he or she is too tired.

Strongly suggested to keep children out of the adult worship service: In some churches, whenever adults with children enter the building, it becomes highly apparent that the greeters/ministry workers are coached to suggest they send their children to the youth service immediately. Sometimes, before a person has found a seat, they will have been offered many times to put his or her children in their youth ministry. Perhaps, the ministry workers are not keeping a record and do not know when they have exhausted the offer.

This invitation is okay. It is excellent that a ministry team is trained to know where to direct people. Many parents who want their children involved in the children's ministry are grateful to know where they can send their children. It just needs to be understood that parents may not want to send their children to the youth ministry until they get comfortable with the church and its ministry workers. Furthermore, what if a child has special needs? Would the typical church youth ministry be prepared to handle that? Hence, parents whose children have special needs should not feel ostracized or overly concerned about having their children remain in the worship service. Parents should know they have the option and that parents, along with their children, are welcome in the church.

Behavioral modification instead of sanctification: Some cultures believe "children are best seen and not heard." However, that type of culture breeds abuse. When children are constantly in an environment where they feel like they are not wanted and their voice is permanently silenced, then when someone truly hurts them, they will not be inclined to report what happened because they know their words will fall on deaf ears. Children have indeed been abused (physically and sexually) by false converts in the church. Children must be seen and heard if we want to lead them to Christ.

Truthfully, there was and perhaps still is a generation of people that grew up in a church and were just told in some form or another to "sit down and shut up." As a result, they never saw church or God as welcoming to their presence. For them, it seemed God, and His people, only tolerated them. As they got older, they left the church, some joined fraternities and sororities; others joined gangs, political groups, cults, or false religions; others started doing witchcraft, having multiple sex partners, and so much more. They got older and sought a community they never had at church as a youth. And their parents are confused because they cannot comprehend how they raised their children to attend church regularly while not wearing a hat or chewing gum, how they sent them to every Christian youth event, yet, they walked away from God the moment they got some independence.

All that happened was that their children had behavioral modification and not authentic sanctification. They were only acting righteous and holy for some time to be pleasing to their parents instead of God. Could such children be saved and, like the prodigal son, are having a backslidden moment? Yes, that is possible. Therefore, parents of backslidden children should pray for their return to the faith.

Nonetheless, the truth is that it is not a bunch of rules that make us pursue a life of holiness and righteousness. The Bible teaches that God's goodness towards people makes one choose Him (Romans 2:4). The scripture teaches that the only reason people can love God is that God loved the people first (1 John 4:19) and filled His people with the Holy Spirit. Once one realizes how merciful and great He has been, then in willful obedience, one submits to God's plan of sanctification for his or her life. It is not the law (Ten Commandments) that saves. It only makes a person behave for a little while. But it was God's grace towards humanity on the cross that provided salvation. Glory be to God! Children need to see the love of God and not just be tolerated. Then when they have trouble as adults, they return to the Church because they have always known it to be a place of grace!

Yes, children need rules, but they also need love. Yes, children can be noisy in a worship service, but stubborn adults should soften their hearts and move closer to the front if they want to hear more clearly. Many churches that only tolerate children often die. One will notice that the churches that do not like children are devoid of them, and as the congregation gets older and passes away, so does their church.

The secular culture is always targeting children. They teach ungodly concepts about relationships, sexuality, finances, and many other subjects. Therefore, we should not ignore children at the church. Children need to be taught the truth at an early age. If society attempts to remove a child's innocence early on, the Church should be the first to take aggressive steps in shaping a child's worldview. I understand there is a time when children cannot be present at all events because of specific reasons, but we must be good to children in the house of God. We have to raise a generation that genuinely loves our God.

DOXOLOGY

Previously, in the section "manners," we talked about all these different "ologies." But what matters most in our interpersonal relationships and the Church at large is our doxology. This is a Greek word having to do with our expression of praise to God —how we praise God matters. In particular, as it relates to this chapter, how we treat other people in God's house can be an expression of praise to God or our inflated egos.

One day, when Christ returns, there will be a great banquet. At this banquet, there will be all sorts of colors, shapes, sizes, and different life experiences (Luke 13:29). We will be sitting at that table because Christ unites us. As difficult as people can be, the people at your church matter to God—they are His—He is their creator and Father. If the people who make up our churches matter to God, they should matter to us.

If one is an excellent visionary leader, he or she will capture this idea of all people mattering to God. The visionary leader will make it clear that relationships matter to God. God is always in the process of making His people reflect more of His kingdom. The Church should never feel like a bunch of individual families coming together and tolerating the other individuals/families there. No, we are the family of God when we gather and even when we scatter. Do not despise the Church. God has proven that He loves His people, even when we fall short.

CHAPTER SEVEN

FINANCIAL STEWARDSHIP

Stewardship is not limited to finances. God calls His people to be good stewards of various aspects of our lives. But I have dedicated an entire chapter to financial stewardship as there has been much confusion surrounding the topic of finances in the Church. Jesus did talk about and require money for His ministry. Jesus had people giving towards His ministry, and Judas was appointed to manage the funds (Luke 8:3, John 12:6).

I, like many others, have witnessed bad ethics concerning money in a worship service. I have seen the collection plate passed around multiple times because the preacher felt the people did not give enough, preachers who demanded a certain amount or the people would not be blessed, and preachers who have physically reached into the purses/wallets of others for money.

As a result of scandals and poor uses of finances within the church, money has become a complex subject to discuss among many Christians. But it does not change the fact that giving is worship. Therefore, is one lousy parent representative of all parents? Should one assume that all marriages fail just because many have? Do people stop driving vehicles because there are car accidents? No! Despite the difficulties, people are still given to marriage, become parents, and drive vehicles, just as giving is still a part of the Church and worship.

The church does need money! We still need to help widows and orphans; we need to support missionary work; we need to support full-time church leaders who dedicate their entire time to building kingdom work (1 Corinthians 9:13-14). Even buildings matter to God. A church is never limited to a building. However, facilities provide security and services for the community and the people of God. Families do better in a building (house), armies prepare better by having buildings (bases), and firefighters do better with a building (fire station). Doctors do better operating on your body in a sterile hospital building. A facility is helpful for groups of people to function.

Likewise, church buildings become places of refuge when communities have been hit by natural disasters. (I.g., churches tend to open their doors for food and shelter.) Church buildings provide a safe environment for the people of God to worship. The church building is a designated space to understand the physical boundaries of protocol. For example, children are not always aware of the dangers of their surroundings. Hence the four walls help to establish safe boundaries or rooms where children can be discipled and expend energy freely. Some churches have community centers/recreational facilities attached to them (playgrounds, babysitting, trade classes) or a cemetery where people have buried their loved ones. No, a church does not need a building to exist, but buildings are valuable and scriptural for us to support having them (1 Kings 5:1-9).

Finances are a part of our worship of God. I only ask the reader to have an open mind as you continue to read this chapter. Suspend your judgments of all the falsehoods concerning money and see the true nature of financial giving.

FINANCIAL GIVING IS WORSHIP

One time David wanted to buy a particular floor for the worship of God. And a person tried to give it to David for free. But David did not want to give anything to God that cost him nothing (2 Samuel 24:24). New Testament believers would sell their homes in support of the ministry (Acts 2:45). When one does not want to give financially, it is a sign that money has a grip on a person more than God does. In the following are two major mental blocks that have stopped Christians from giving:

Hypocrites: Luke 4:16 reads: "*He went to Nazareth, where he had been brought up, and on the Sabbath day he went into the synagogue, **as was his custom**"* (emphasis mine). Ponder this for a moment. Jesus went to the synagogue/church regularly! He habitually went to the place where pharisees would gather and worship. He even did not stop people from giving money to the temple. But instead, He acknowledged and celebrated a woman who gave out of her lack (Mark 12:41-44). So wait a minute! Jesus continued to go to church with hypocritical church leaders (pharisees). He also was not opposed to supporting the temple financially. Not only did He encourage people to give money to the temple, but He also led as an example by contributing monetarily to the temple (Matthew 17:24-27).

Tithing: Tithing is a principle of worship, not a law. The law was only installed to enforce principles people refused to live by. For example, an intrinsic principle among human beings is that life matters—especially human life. However, when a person becomes self-centered, he or she may drive at excessive speeds, disregard yield signs, drive through red lights, and the like; without considering how other people could get hurt. Therefore, there are laws to discourage such practices.

Likewise, by principle, human beings should desire to love their creator and His creation. We should be courteous to others and show thankfulness to our God. However, due to sin, humanity struggles to acknowledge their God and respect His creation. So God instituted the law (Ten Commandments and other commands) to remind us of the principles of love, respect, and other virtues. Because we could not live by godly principles, God gave us the law—to show us our errors and point us to Christ (Romans 3:20). Hence, tithing, a principle of virtue, was added to the law by God to get self-centered people to be generous. (Leviticus 27:30).

God prefers people to give from love, admiration, and thankfulness—not because someone is forced to. Tithing, from its inception, had nothing to do with legalism or the law. It is a practice/principle where people demonstrate their love for God. It is the belief that God is ultimately the Christian's provider. Therefore, Christians give God a tenth of their income to demonstrate their trust in God's ability to provide for His people.

The law was introduced in the time of Moses. And yet, patriarchs such as Abraham and Jacob, who predated Moses, cheerfully gave God a tenth of their increase:

*Then Melchizedek king of Salem brought out bread and wine. He was priest of God Most High, and he blessed Abram, saying, 'Blessed be Abram by God Most High, Creator of heaven and earth. And praise be to God Most High, who delivered your enemies into your hand.' Then Abram gave him a **tenth** of everything.* (Genesis 14:18-20, emphasis mine)

*Then Jacob made a vow, saying, 'If God will be with me and will watch over me on this journey I am taking and will give me food to eat and clothes to wear so that I return safely to my father's household, then the Lord will be my God and this stone that I have set up as a pillar will be God's house, and of all that you give me **I will give you a tenth**.'* (Genesis 28:20-22, emphasis mine)

Notice how Abraham and Jacob gave out of thankfulness to God. Melchizedek was the priest and therefore represented God. So Abraham gave his tenth to Melchizedek, just like we give a tenth to our local church. It is physically handed to a person/ people but in faith towards God. They did not give financially because of a law forcing them. They were unselfish and grateful.

Furthermore, when Jesus mentions tithing in the gospel narrative, He does not discourage it. He says not to neglect to tithe but to keep in line with the weightier matters, for He says, *"Woe to you, teachers of the law and Pharisees, you hypocrites! You give a tenth of your spices—mint, dill and cumin. But you have neglected the more important matters of the law—justice, mercy and faithfulness. You should have practiced the latter, **without neglecting the former**"* (Matthew 23:23, emphasis mine).

If tithing was tied to the law of the Old Covenant, why did Christ not discourage it here? Why did He say not to "neglect" it? He references tithing, justice, mercy, and faithfulness as the "law" because that was the language understood by the pharisees. But these subjects were always a principle/practice of love, in which all the law rested (Matthew 22:34-40). The practice of tithing comes from one's admiration towards God so that God's house has resources for ministers and ministries (Numbers 18:21, Nehemiah 13:10-13). Tithing remained in the New Testament because it is a principle/practice that predates and transcends the OT law. Again, Abraham and Jacob (pre-law) tithed, not out of fearfulness to a law but from a joyful heart.

ROBBING GOD

So what does one do with Malachi 3:6-9? In summary, God states that Israel had not adhered to His command because they had not been tithing and offering. He wants them to bring the whole tithe and offering into His "house." Furthermore, He calls Israel robbers for withholding. God goes as far as to say that their entire nation is cursed because they do not give tithes and offerings.

Where else in scripture do we hear God referring to His people as "robbers," concerning His "house"? Jesus entered a temple that was supposed to be a "house of prayer," but He called it a "den of robbers." The temple had become a marketplace instead of a proper place of worship. One could infer that greed was the issue. However, the main reason Christ was upset is that prayer was nullified! The money took the place of worship (Matthew 21:13). Prayer connects a person with God. And yet, money served as a distraction to prayer. Money in itself is not inherently evil, but the admiration and worship of it are. They were actually "robbing" glory from God.

Why is God upset in the book of Malachi? Because the people prized and loved their resources (money) more than God. They trusted in their resources more than God because they held onto them. However, if they understood the glory of God and how great He is, by the principle of Him being a generous God, they, too, would be generous. Furthermore, they would practice tithes and offerings because they know everything comes from God—if God asks people for something, it is because He has something better in mind to exchange with them. So why is one cursed when one does not tithe and offer? Because any nation whose god is their resource or money is under a curse.

Money is a social construct. Meaning that it only has value because people say it does. How, then, can money compete with God? Who gave God His value? The answer is no one! He has existed before time. The value of money can increase or decrease over time. But God remains the same. He does not change, for He is from everlasting to everlasting. His value is intrinsic. So yes, when money has one's heart more than God, that person or nation is under a curse. The Bible teaches that the source of all evil is the love of money (1 Timothy 6:10). Jesus said you could not serve God and money (Luke 16:13). He said, *"For where your treasure is, there your heart will be also"* (Matthew 6:21).

In short, money never satisfies. One always needs more of it. And this is the curse of having money as your god. If a person works hard for it, that person might still lose it. People worry about if they can pay their bills. Yet, when one trusts God as a provider, one knows He will never disappoint. If a person does not tithe and offer, will God still care for that person's needs? Yes, Jehovah is a benevolent and compassionate God. But when people do not submit their finances, there will always be a sense of not having enough. People feel restless as they attempt to be a provider for themselves.

In contrast, God offers rest to those who do it His way (Hebrews 4:1-3). Without a doubt, Christians are not under the Old Covenant anymore. God has given people this time of grace called the New Covenant. Nonetheless, this life is still under a curse. Bodies still get old and die; disease is rampant, and hard work is still necessary! Therefore, Christians find peace amid chaos by entrusting themselves to God in all things about life and death, including finances.

GIVING OUTLETS

Within the Bible, there are different kinds of giving:

First Fruits: This was when people gave the first and best of their initial yield/flock (Proverbs 3:9). Able gave a first fruit offering when he gave the best of his flock to God. Jesus is referred to in the Bible as a First fruit offering (1 Corinthians

15:20). Meaning that God offered His best and first Son to the world.

First fruits was an annual (one-time) offering. Because the modern economy is not primarily based on agriculture, a first fruit offering equivalent will be different for everyone depending on the circumstance. For example, some offer their tax refund yearly as a first fruit offering. Or if one receives a pay increase, that person can take the initial percentage and give it to God.

Alms: Christians are encouraged to give to the destitute (1 John 3:17, Matthew 5:42). How much will be determined by the need and what God is leading a person to do at the moment. A lame man once asked for money, but Peter and John gave him something far better than money. They commanded the man's legs to be healed, and they were (Acts 3:1-10).

Seed Offering: This is a free-will offering that may or may not be given directly to your church (the tithe is designated to your local church). The seed offering can be assigned to a ministry or person outside of your local church. However, it is not limited to a specific financial amount. This offering is about reaping what you have sown into others (Galatians 6:7). Moreover, because of God's grace and goodness, the harvest can be even greater than what was sown. Jesus stated, "*Give, and it will be given to you. A good measure, pressed down, shaken together and running over, will be poured into your lap. For with the measure you use, it will be measured to you*" (Luke 6:38). Whatever you give, God promises to bless you abundantly for it (2 Corinthians 9:6).

Tithing: Tithing differs from the previously listed offerings in that there is a prescribed amount of ten percent. Tithing was/is the regular giving one gives to God's local storehouse/church

(Malachi 3:10). God instructed the Israelites to give a tenth of all their crops to God (Deuteronomy 14:22)—every time there was a yield, ten percent went to God. This recurring financial giving was a reminder to be thankful to God for providing all things. Whether a person practices the regular giving of tithing or one of the offerings mentioned, God blesses His children for their giving (Malachi 3:8-12).

There is one more giving option that I did not include in the previous list—**giving it all**. And I wanted to have this last giving principle at the end as it is the most difficult. Christ told the Rich Young Ruler to sell all his possessions before following Him (Luke 18:18-30). Jesus celebrated the poor widow, who gave the last of her money to the temple, while everyone else was giving from their abundance—she gave everything (Mark 12:43-44)! People struggle to believe that God would ask them to give everything, whereas one needs to remember this is the same God that told Abraham to sacrifice his son, Isaac (Genesis 22:2). But did Isaac die? No, God was only testing Abraham's faithfulness. Likewise, had the Rich Young Ruler not sadly walked away from Christ's request to sell everything, he would have heard of the rewards for his obedience. "*Truly I tell you, 'Jesus said to them, 'no one who has left home or wife or brothers or sisters or parents or children for the sake of the kingdom of God will fail to receive many times as much in this age, and in the age to come eternal life*'" (Luke 18:29-30).

Furthermore, those early believers in the book of Acts did not believe they owned their possessions—they shared everything they had. They would sell their lands and houses for the ministry (Acts 4:32-35). As one can see, the New Testament believers were radical in their giving. They were not limited to the tithe; they went beyond it and gave sacrificially.

So if one wants to limit the principle/practice of tithing to the Old Testament law, then the next option is to give all or sacrificially as they did in the New Testament book of Acts. If the highest form of financial giving in the New Testament was giving all, could God get that sacrificial offering from the modern believer? Would one prefer to give a tithe or to give everything as many New Testament believers did?

The truth of the scripture is clear, God does invite us to give. God believes that He is worth our giving and has promised to bless us for our contribution—blessings in this life and the next. Does this mean you will be a millionaire? The Bible states that Abraham was extremely rich (Genesis 13:2). But that does not mean all people will be immensely rich. It does mean God will take care of you. Every good parent wants to care for their children and even bless them beyond basic needs.

People give to what they believe in. People give money to soda companies even though it promotes obesity and diabetes. People make the movie industry rich by supporting movies, even though many films do not support Christian values. People fatten the wallets of many political campaigns even though many American politicians are only conveniently Christian. People financially support car companies, food products, clothing products, and many others. Even if the founders and ethics of such companies are corrupt, we support their products/ services because they enhance our lives. What I am saying is this: most people can tithe and offer, but they give that money to something or someone else. And God sees when one values other things over His kingdom.

* *Some Christians will use the Apostle Paul's statement to negate tithing. He states, "Each of you should **give what you have decided in your heart** to give, not reluctantly or under compulsion, for God loves a cheerful giver (2 Corinthians 9:7, emphasis mine). However, this was about a seed offering, a free-will offering one makes toward God's work. Ministers are coming to assist the church in Corinth. And Paul is ensuring its*

members accommodate their stay financially while they are with them. Paul only asks them to make good on what they had already promised. People told Paul that they would financially take care of him and his associates if they had come (2 Corinthians 9:5). Paul was encouraging them to keep their promise. Tithing was still a regular practice in the New Testament, and this was a seed offering the church at Corinth volunteered. Since it was volunteered and not a part of the regular giving, the members could give as each had "decided."

WHAT ABOUT THE POOR?

What about the widows and the poor? Should they make an offering? The Bible seems to think so. The widow at Zarephath gave her last meal to Elijah. She chose to feed a prophet instead of her child because of the instruction of God! As a result, God blessed her supernaturally and provided plenty of food for her (1 Kings 17:7-16). In other words, there are times when perhaps people cannot give (not even one penny), but God does ask people to give sacrificially—even a widow. And God blessed this woman beyond measure. While others were struggling during a drought and famine, God took care of her because she obeyed the instruction of giving.

Are there fakes and phonies concerning money within the church? Without a doubt, yes! But is God's word still valid? YES, IT IS! We should trust God with our giving. We should do it cheerfully when we place money in the offering bucket. Even if someone does something unethical with money, God's sovereignty will always win! His kingdom will advance, and He will reward and celebrate those for making His work important. In a misguided attempt to prove one's piety, one might say, "I don't care if God rewards me for my giving." And any such person is welcome to think that way. Nevertheless, God loves

His people and will reward us for our giving, whether we agree with rewards for giving or not. You will not loose your salvation because you do not give. And God will not love you more because you give. The good news is that in God's sovereignty, He cannot love you any more tomorrow than He already does presently. It is an unchanging and everlasting love—you cannot change that. However, I do not want to stand before God and hear Him say, "There were many people, building projects, ministries, and missions that were delayed, because when I asked you to give...you did not." God loves us, and He will judge us according to our works. May you receive your full reward because of your obedience. May you be found faithful with the treasure you have been given. Amen.

CHAPTER EIGHT

TITLES MATTER

What title comes to mind when one hears of a woman breastfeeding, dressing, and reading stories to a child? What title comes to mind when a person is wearing a particular uniform with a utility belt holding a gun, chases, and arrests those violating the law? What title comes to mind when a person is wearing a white coat, washing his or her hands vigorously several times a day, using a scalpel to perform surgeries, and prescribing medicine? If one thinks correctly, the answer to all these questions in the order they were presented would be a mother, a police officer, and a medical doctor.

The reason one can attribute titles to said persons is because of the function they performed. In other words, titles represent functions. When one goes to a house or business to fix plumbing issues for pay, one automatically calls that person a "plumber." When someone has been drastically injured in a public space, the bystanders do not yell, "Is there a motivational speaker, barista, or a carpenter that can help!" No, they ask for the assistance of a medical doctor. Why? Because the specific title asked for can perform the function or task necessary for the situation.

Imagine an emergency at a person's home, and this person calls a random number. When the stranger answers the phone, the person needing assistance says, "Help, my house is on fire; I need you to come over and put the fire out." Naturally, one knows this is foolish since the stranger receiving the phone call could be several miles away and may not have the tools or skills necessary to help the person in need. Instinctively, in the United States, people know that one only needs to call the emergency number (911). And the person who functions as a liaison with the title of "dispatcher" will send people who have the function to put out fires which are called "firefighters."

This is all to say that titles do matter. Even scripturally, one knows this to be true. Jesus was a common name in biblical times. But only one had the title "Christ" attached to His name. Christ means "anointed one," "Messiah," or "king." Throughout Jesus' ministry, many speculated about if He was Christ. They would see and hear what He was doing; they would experience the function of Christ. And while many theorized who He was, others rightly discerned He was the Christ. The Christian knows that what distinguishes Jesus from other religious figureheads is that He was the "anointed one" of God. He truly is the Son of God. And it is by His name/title that one is saved (Acts 4:12).

God, Himself has established titles for a reason. Christians should not get into the habit of believing titles do not matter. In particular, this chapter will show the importance of the visionary leader's title.

THE RESPONSIBILITY OF RELATIONSHIP

Relationships naturally come with a responsibility or burden. And it is the title of every relationship that invokes the depth of meaning and commitment the relationship entails. For example, the following is a list of relationship titles, and each one has its sense of responsibility:

Friend
Wife or husband
Boss
Enemy
Mother or father

Counselor
Stranger
Benefactor

Which of these titles naturally provides comfort? What title is the most intimidating? Out of all these titles, which is the most burdensome? Depending on the perspective, some of these titles have more responsibility than others. For instance, the title "boss" can affect a person in several ways. A boss puts a burden on the employee, or a person who is the boss has to deal with the burdens of administrative duties. The point is that every relational title comes with a responsibility. This is why some people pursue shallow relationships or want as few relationships as possible. Because to be in a relationship means one has to use time and energy to sustain it.

Consider the responsibility or burden placed on people that wanted to follow or be connected to certain biblical leaders. To follow Abraham meant to follow a man who did not even have a direct location in mind. Later, when Isaac followed his father Abraham up a mountain, he had no idea his father was prepared to sacrifice him. One had to leave their family behind to follow Elijah without saying "goodbye." Following Noah meant accepting that many other loved ones and acquaintances would be left behind and subjected to death without recourse. To follow the Apostle Paul meant one had to be among dangerous elements and people. To follow Jesus means to pick your cross (live a sacrificial life) and continue to follow Him all the days of your life. Jesus would command people to sell all their possessions (Mark 10:21), not to attend family members' funerals (Matthew 8:22), and to die for His cause (John 21:19)!

When the Prophet Samuel appeared to anoint David as king of Israel, the town's elders trembled at Samuel's presence. While Samuel was there for something positive, the people understood that Samuel's title as a "prophet" could render a blessing or a curse (1 Samuel 16:4). Moreover, Cain did not want to be responsible for his brother Able. By nature of the relationship alone—siblings—God wanted Cain to be a better keeper of that relationship (Genesis 4:9). Every relationship has a title to describe the functions of the relationship. And each title bestows a blessing or curse—sometimes both.

The responsibility of a title affects the person with the title and the one who receives the function from the person with the title. And the one who bears the title will have to handle a weightier burden. However, one will transition from a man to a husband, from employee to employer, because one believes the rewards outweigh the disadvantages of never attaining those higher stations. Likewise, there is a burden to becoming a Christian. The world will reject Christians. But Jesus also promised that the burdens would not become overbearing so long as a Christian stays connected to Him (Matthew 11:30).

There is a responsibility visionary leaders must take on when they are addressed by their title. Be it an apostle, prophet, pastor, or other, it does come with a responsibility. And the congregational members who accept their visionary leader's position in their life are subject to the guidance or leadership of the one with the function of said title. Unfortunately, I assert that many believers struggle to submit to their visionary leader's authority even though God made the leader authoritative.

However, this is no different from being subjected to an airplane pilot. One does not know the pilot's personal history, mindset, or capability. What if the pilot was suicidal while operating the plane? What if the pilot gets drunk while steering the plane? And yet, one willingly subjects themselves to a pilot's expertise, trusting that the pilot will get them to the destination safely. This is just one of the many examples where humans subject themselves to someone else's leadership.

Therefore, one has to be willing to trust the visionary leader God has placed in his or her life if one truly wants the benefits of that relationship. As the pilot expects financial gain from the passengers, and the passengers accept the pilot's expertise, they both benefit. In the same manner, when done correctly, the responsibility of the relationship between a church leader and congregational members will be mutually beneficial, and the kingdom of God will advance.

ACCESS

As previously alluded to, titles/names are like doors to opportunities or detriments. The name Satan means "accuser." There will be some accusation or condemnation whenever Satan is involved. The doorway of Satan will always be filled with division, devastation, and destruction. Because of the accusatory nature of Satan, one can be sure that opening his door or gate will lead you to shame and death (Matthew 7:13).

On the contrary, the name Jesus means to "rescue" or "save." When Jesus is in a person's life, He will rescue that person from every false accusation and malicious scheme against the person. Even when one has done wrong, Jesus provides the opportunity for repentance and forgiveness so that whatever sin one has committed, in the eyes of God, it will be as if it never happened after one accepts the Gospel message. People may not forgive you, but Jesus will because He saves! Jesus claimed to be a doorway (gate) to life (John 10:9).

Titles give you access, but ignorance or dishonor will keep a person from reaping the benefits of a title. For instance, when a married couple is in an argument. And the exchange becomes too intense. One spouse may say to the other, "Don't talk to me like that...I am your wife/husband." The spouse has concluded that the title of wife or husband requires honorable discussion. And when the conversation does not change to a respectful tone, one or both parties will shut down emotionally—leaving the relationship without joy for a season until reconciliation happens.

The woman at the well in John 4 addressed Jesus as a "prophet" and "Messiah." Therefore she received that ministry; blind Bartimaeus received Jesus as the "Son of David," which was a messianic title meaning that Jesus was a descendant of King David and would be a deliverer like David was. Therefore, Bartimaeus was "delivered" from his blindness (Luke 18:35-43). Commander Naaman was cured of his leprosy because he received Elisha as a prophet (2 Kings 5:14).

Imagine if Nicodemus had been disrespectful. Would he have gotten a response from Jesus? There were times when religious leaders and those in authority would seek answers from the Lord, but He would give rhetorical answers or not respond because they were dishonorable. However, when Nicodemus approached Jesus, he addressed Him as "rabbi." This is significant because Nicodemus was considered Israel's most outstanding teacher (rabbi) at the time. Yet, he needed Jesus to teach him, so he addressed him as a teacher (John 3:1-15). Jesus even said it was good that His disciples addressed Him as a teacher (John 13:13). Hence, the result is that Jesus spent time with Nicodemus by giving him a lesson on what it means to be born again (John 13:13-14).

Every biblical title comes with blessings attached to it (fivefold ministers, elders, deacons, and others). The characters in the Bible that were given titles only received those titles to be a blessing to God's people. The Church needed more workers to help take care of widows, so the apostles anointed people with the title of "deacon" to serve. Hence, the titles of visionary leaders (bishop, apostle, and more) and other leaders supporting the visionary leader all matter for your benefit. They give you access to the provision of God.

BOUNDARIES

Titles instantly create boundaries. The single man knows he should not show romantic interest in a married woman, for she has the title of wife. The employee knows to rely on the manager for final decisions. Titles always point to the extent to which someone has jurisdiction. This is why God is called the "Alpha and Omega," or when Moses asks for His name, God states, "I am, that I am." In other words, God is from everlasting to everlasting. There are no boundaries for God. All that there is and will be, God owns. All creation exists within the bounds He created. Any attempt to subvert His boundaries is called sin or a transgression.

Even earthly relationships require boundaries. A relationship without boundaries is called abuse. What makes a murderer a murderer? What makes a spouse commit infidelity? There are many reasons one could give for these questions. But primarily, murder and adultery result from someone stepping over the boundaries. The point is that titles create boundaries. And where there are no titles and people that respect titles, there will be abuse. Hence, the visionary leader's title must be maintained to create healthy relational boundaries. Of course, there are those with titles who abuse power. And we correct, discipline, or remove those that do. Nonetheless, a title is important.

The mistake Christians make is to approach and interact with the visionary leader like a casual friend. To the detriment of the congregation, the visionary leader is addressed or reduced to a "dude" or "buddy" type of relationship. How does one define the relationship if the visionary leader is addressed and treated more like a friend than a leader? What boundaries are there?

Depending on a given situation, a person's friend might be of consequence. But leaders within their jurisdiction must always be of consequence. A friend shares a suggestion, but a leader gives direction—therefore, when a leader is reduced to the "friend zone", they are of no benefit to the people they are supposed to be leading. Leaders like Moses and Jeremiah did not have many friends. And often, the people they were leading turned on them. But they were effective leaders in what God asked them to do. Leaders can be friendly, but to do their job effectively, they cannot be everyone's friend.

Does one need a police officer to be his or her friend? What if you had an emergency and the police officer said, "I cannot help you because you're not my friend!." That would be an outrage! One expects police officers to help them regardless of friendship status. They have the title of "police officer," which makes them obligated to help citizens in their jurisdiction. One would expect police officers to defend the constitutional rights of the American people, not because of friendship, but because their title implies they swore an oath to do so! The title of "friend" is subjective. Its definition changes depending on those involved. But a title such as "police officer" is objective. There are governing principles for how the officer and the citizen are to interact with one another. For the safety of the police and the citizens, law enforcement must have recognized titles and badges, as it reminds us of the boundaries. The title helps keep everyone accountable.

Perhaps in some congregations, it is acceptable to address the visionary leader by the first name only. It certainly is not a sin to do so if done respectfully. But not everyone who comes to church is going to be respectful. That is why it is wise to address and interact with the visionary leader with the title they possess. If the visionary leader is called an apostle, one should address that person as an apostle. If the title is evangelist, one should address that person with that designation. Perhaps in times past, one of the reasons there have been sex and money scandals in God's house is because the leader, as well as the people, have reduced the visionary leader's title and role to that of a friend. A "friend" is too loose of a title for such an important role—leading God's house. Visionary leaders must be objective in their approach to ministry. Nothing articulates that better than when they are addressed with their title.

Over time, some people can develop a friendship with the visionary leader. Jonathan and David were undoubtedly friends. However, Jonathan still had respect for who David was. Nonetheless, I believe too many church members want to pursue a friendship with visionary leaders without first submitting to their leadership. The reason you follow a leader is that you need his or her leadership! Imagine that 50 to 300 people are attempting to be your friend simultaneously. Could you weekly and effectively spend an hour on the phone with each person? Could you weekly and effectively visit each one at their house? Could you laugh and have small talk consistently with all of them? The answer is an overwhelming no! Some people would resent you because you might only be able to spend time with two or three of the many people you claim as your friend. What about your family? After you try to be emotionally and physically available to those 50 to 300 friends, would you have anything left for your spouse and children? Would there be enough time left for prayer and devotion to God?

In other words, the visionary leader cannot possibly be everyone's friend at a church. But the leader can pray for you, have office hours for a counseling session, and do Bible studies that people can attend. In short, some people have misunderstood the role of their visionary leader. And even visionary leaders have sometimes misunderstood their role and tried to be everyone's friend, only to fail. So, when the members cannot develop a friendship with the leader, they are disappointed. However, your visionary leader can still truly develop, guide, direct, and even love you without having a close friendship. No doubt, the Bible says that Jesus called His disciples friend, and we are His friends. But as a human, He limited deeper fellowship to the twelve disciples. However, because He is also God, He can supernaturally be our friend simultaneously (John 15:15)! But your visionary leader is a human being who cannot be everywhere at one time and has limited energy.

SPIRITUAL FATHERS

The idea of being a spiritual father (or mother) is a genuine concept in the Bible and applies today. However, the idea has been gravely mistaken. As a result, people claim to be spiritual fathers who are not truly qualified. And people are looking to get a spiritual father because they think they are incomplete without one. The following is an attempt to make biblical sense of this title:

Apostles and Prophets are spiritual fathers: Spiritual paternity in the Bible was always done by someone in an authoritative office. That would be someone who meets the qualification of a biblical elder but also has a governing office within the Church (fivefold ministers). Typically, whenever one is addressed as a spiritual father in the Bible, it is usually an apostle or prophet. The Apostle Paul claimed to be Timothy's father and the father of the Galatian church (1 Corinthians 4:17, Galatians 4:19). Elisha addressed the Prophet Elijah as his father (2 Kings 2:12). One could say the priest had a role in "fathering" as the priest Eli was to Samuel. Or a teacher has a role in fathering as Nicodemus "fathered" the understanding of God for all of Israel. And, of course, the patriarchs and kings were regarded as spiritual fathers. The point still withstanding, these were people that had the authority of an office and leadership over God's people.

Hence, this is not done by church members or any other office outside of the governmental offices. Believers such as deacons, Bible study leaders, outreach leaders, youth workers, and the like can undoubtedly help to inspire, coach, and guide other believers, but building one's foundational understanding is left for the governmental offices of the Church. Scripture even said that the New Testament believers submitted to the doctrine as taught by the apostles. So if one were without an office and taught various subjects, it would have stemmed from the foundational message the apostles laid (Acts 2:42).

Spiritual fathers build the foundation: The reason apostles and prophets primarily do the fathering is that scripture claims them to be foundational to the Church (Ephesians 2:20). Earthly parents give us a footing. A lot of what people have learned and the habits they display come directly from their parents. Ideally, earthly parents are mature enough to raise a child. In so doing, they help their child start well in life. A child may have school teachers, babysitters, sports coaches, therapists, or mentors that help the child along. But all these additional helpers are complementary to the foundation already established by the parents. The same is true of spiritual parents. The Apostle Paul said to the Corinthian church, *"Even if you had ten thousand guardians in Christ, you do not have many fathers, for in Christ Jesus I became your father through the gospel"* (1 Corinthians 4:15). Spiritual parenting is for those mature governmental ministers. It is not for immature Christians or new converts (1 Timothy 3:6).

Spiritual parents are an added benefit but not a requirement: One does not have to retain a spiritual father to validate his or her ministry. When the Prophet Amos came along, he claimed to have no spiritual father. He did not have someone to lay a foundation for him. If someone did, it is not recorded in scripture. Amos asserted that he worked as a farmer when God called him to prophesy and had no formal prophetic training (Amos 7:14-15).

The Prophet Amos may not have had a spiritual father, but he has accountability and affirmation in that the Church has affirmed his message by including it in the Bible. That is to say that accountability is necessary for all believers. It would have been great if someone could have affirmed Amos in his day. Even the Prophet Elijah had a man named Obadiah that supported him in his ministry. But Amos is one of those rare ministers of the Old Testament who had to pioneer a message that people did not embrace immediately.

Nonetheless, the Church must have elders partly for accountability. Jesus even said that when a dispute is not settled between believers, the church (elders, fivefold ministers) should evaluate it (Matthew 18:15-17). Mature believers are needed to test and see if decisions and declarations are from God or not (1 John 4:1). Accountability is necessary, but a personal spiritual father is not.

While joining a local assembly is not a requirement for salvation, it is an act of obedience. Believers do need to belong to a church. Believers need a fivefold minister in their life for accountability and guidance. Even fivefold ministers need other fivefold ministers for accountability. Nevertheless, if you do not have a spiritual father, it does not mean you have to look for one. But should a real spiritual father or mother be a part of your life, it will expedite your growth and promote you. The Prophet Elijah had many students/spiritual children. However, he only had one that genuinely distinguished himself as a spiritual son—His name was Elisha, and he got a double portion of Elijah's mantle.

Furthermore, are we allowed to call other ministers fathers? Some have questioned if Christians are permitted to claim people as spiritual fathers because Jesus said to call no one on earth your father since God is your father (Matthew 23:9). But one must use scripture to interpret scripture. Hence, as we compare and contrast this statement to other scripture, one should gain a better understanding. David called Saul his father (1 Samuel 24:11). The Apostle Paul referred to himself as a father. Abraham is recognized as the father of our faith (Galatians 3:6-9).

Moreover, in verse 8 of Matthew 23, Jesus stated that we should not call anyone father or teacher. And yet, Solomon was referred to as a wise teacher (Ecclesiastes 12:9). Also, 1 Corinthians 12:28 claims that God has appointed teachers! So how can Jesus tell us not to call anyone teacher or father, and yet scripture, God's word in both the New and Old Testament, confirms and affirms those terms when referring to people?

The answer is that these terms, when used for people, are meant to be representative of but not the replacement of God. That is why the Apostle Paul would tell people to follow him but only as he was led by Christ (1 Corinthians 11:1). You can have natural and spiritual teachers and parents, but one is not to turn those people into idols. Teachers and parents are meant to lead us to Christ, not deter us from Him. That was the case when people started to worship King Herod. The people claimed he had the voice of God. And when he did not attribute his wisdom to the real God, God killed him on the spot (Acts 12:23). The problem was not his being recognized as an earthly king; it was when he allowed people to think he was the King of kings—there is only one. Glory be to the Lamb of God!

Direct Message for Current Spiritual Fathers

I want to take a moment and speak directly to those that are spiritual fathers and mothers whose spiritual children are serving churches and ministries outside of the authority of the spiritual parents. Your spiritual children must submit to and support the local church or ministry to which they belong. The spiritual children of the Prophet Elijah will function differently than the spiritual children of the Prophet Samuel. Elijah is a mighty prophet who called down fire and fought the prophets of Baal. In comparison, Samuel is more regal and, at times, more diplomatic.

Even though Elijah and Samuel existed in different periods, imagine a student from the pedigree of Elijah attempting to follow Samuel. Would that student need to change? Would not that student have to adjust to the teaching, principles, and revelation that were given to Samuel? Undoubtedly, what that student received from Elijah is excellent, and much would remain. Yet, this particular student would need to adjust to the revelation and style of Samuel.

If this student were to compare Samuel to Elijah regularly, it would become a distraction—it would be disrespectful to Samuel. If every time Samuel tried to give new information to this student, the student would cancel out what was said by consulting with Elijah; Samuel would feel as if he was wasting his time with a pupil that does not want his teaching.

The transition from one teacher to another happened in the Bible. The disciples of John the Baptist began to leave him to follow Jesus. John only offered baptism with water, but Jesus would give them the baptism of fire. To stay with John, while good, would limit their growth. So, as his disciples left him to follow Jesus, he said, "...He must become greater; I must become less" (John 3:30). This is the heart of any real spiritual father. They want their spiritual children to become greater than themselves. John knew their next season was with Jesus. And he did not stunt their growth, but he let them grow up.

Just like earthly children, spiritual children grow up. As a spiritual father, you have placed many good things in them. You gave them a great foundation, and you can remain a part of your spiritual children's lives. But please, if your spiritual children have moved on to another church or ministry that is not your own, do not allow your influence to sabotage a church or ministry that has a different mission than yours. Let your children grow up and be promoted. Of course, parents appreciate and enjoy the children that give a phone call and visit.

Nonetheless, as children grow up, you cannot keep them in an infantile state. They will take on new friends, mentors, and opportunities, get married and produce their own children. They take what you have given them in a new direction that may not be bad but is different from what you expected.

Sometimes people leave spiritual coverings or leaders behind for the wrong reasons; they may struggle to submit to any real authority, and they never grow the way God intended. However, there are times when the reason God sent your spiritual children to a new mission field outside of your authority is that God is promoting them in a new way. Your spiritual children have taken on a new wineskin for the new wine God is about to pour out. Celebrate your spiritual children and tell them to fully submit and engage with a new leader or direction in their life.

HONOR

Imagine attending the barbecue of a friend named Mark, who is a judge. Mark is a longtime childhood friend whom you have affectionately nicknamed "Waffle." You call him this because when he was a child, all he wanted to do was eat waffles. You could always find Mark desiring or eating waffles for breakfast, lunch, or dinner.

While you are in the backyard eating good food and laughing, you tell Mark how you would like to see him presiding over a court case. He informs you of a court case that you can attend tomorrow. Watching your friend rule over the case, you were highly impressed. When the case comes to a close, you approach Mark and yell loudly, "Great job, Waffle!" Many of those in attendance, including Mark's interns and colleagues, hear you address him this way while he is still wearing his robe and in the function of a judge.

Mark may be called "Waffle" at the barbecue, but in the courtroom, where he is an authority, he should be recognized as "your Honor" or addressed as "Judge," followed by his last name. Even addressing him as "Mark" without his title and proceeding with his first name would be dishonorable in a courtroom setting. His parents, siblings, friends, and colleagues call him that because they know him personally. But in a courtroom where he is dealing with criminals who do not know him personally, addressing him as "judge" or "your Honor" is appropriate and sets the parameters for his reason for being there. "Mark" is not descriptive enough for a courtroom setting. One has to know where the authority lies. And addressing him only as "Mark" does not speak to his role in the courtroom. Additionally, addressing him as "Waffle" is embarrassing. No one can take a person seriously who is called "Waffle."

Likewise, it is always best to address people by their title unless the individual tells you otherwise. Whether it is the visionary leader or other people holding a position in the Church, always start with recognizing their position. A title has nothing to do with arrogance, even though some arrogant men have titles. No, a title should humble the people who have one. It should make them like a servant. When people are unwilling to address someone with the appropriate title in the proper setting, it is because they are dishonorable. Indeed, titles do not make the man or woman. But there is a reason that man or woman has the title. If God has placed a title upon a man or woman, they have a big responsibility. And Jesus even told His disciples, "*Whoever listens to you listens to me; whoever rejects you rejects me; but whoever rejects me rejects him who sent me"* (Luke 10:16). Sometimes, people do not realize that when we fail to honor others, we fail to honor Christ.

CHAPTER NINE

HONORING LEADERS

Everyone needs leaders. Even leaders need leaders. Leaders are people who make it easier for others to fulfill their call. What they say and do becomes the pattern of success for others. They are wise, stable, decisive, bold, and courageous. They build the foundation. When they win, they share the glory with everyone, and when they lose, they take the blame themselves. That is what Jesus modeled for us. His victory over sin became our victory! We became sons and daughters of God because of what He did. However, the sins of the world He took on by Himself. We share in His victory, but He died and took on the shame of the many. No one can know the sacrifice of a visionary leader until they have been one themselves. Even still, each visionary leader is unique and must live at a different level of sacrifice depending on the mission.

In every aspect of life, leaders have always been necessary for advancement. As it relates to the Church, God wants His people to yield to the ones He has placed in charge. The scripture states, "*Have confidence in your leaders and* **submit to their authority**, *because they keep watch over you as those who must give an account. Do this so that their work will be a joy, not a burden, for that would be of no* **benefit** *to you*" (Hebrews 13:17, emphasis mine).

Submission is a part of life. If one knows anything, it is because one has submitted to a system or authority for learning. You are reading this book today because someone taught you to read. People are taught mathematics, the rules of driving a vehicle, and much more. Nature itself is an authority to which one must submit. Regardless of how one feels, people know that gravity, wind, water, and fire can be dangerous if improperly engaged.

We submit by eating food from people we do not know at restaurants, trusting that what has been offered will not be poisoned. We submit by getting into buses and taxicabs, hoping the drivers safely get us to our destination. We submit by allowing surgeons to place us under anesthetic and operate on our bodies while believing we will not die. We do these things because while there are risks, there are also benefits. We experience the luxury and nourishment of food being prepared for us; we have the convenience of not having to walk due to public transit; and the vitality of our lives is extended through the hands of the surgeon. So why does the body of Christ struggle to submit to the Church and its leaders? Indeed, people have paid for food poisoning at restaurants, died on public transit, and have had harmful or fatal surgical experiences. And yet, people continue to trust these entities. Why? Because the reward outweighs the risk. It is risky to have a brain tumor removed, but people do it because their lives will be cut short without the surgery. And if the surgery happens without fault, the reward is more time with loved ones and friends.

Unfortunately, the Devil has deceived many into believing that Christian leaders are just too risky and that people are better off without them. Even though God has ordained Christian leadership, some Christians do not understand the importance of leadership, so they get into the sin of rebellion. As one will realize in the next chapter, rebellious people want to keep others accountable without themselves being accountable. Even when they have a leader, it is often just a figurehead, a "yes man" (2 Timothy 3:5), who is not close enough to them, nor do they want the leader close enough, to evaluate and discern what they are like. Therefore they are not held accountable. Lucifer also wanted no accountability for his actions. And one cannot reap the benefits that God placed within a leader if they are not genuinely receptive to the leader.

BENEFITS

As alluded to in the previous section, the writer of Hebrews strongly emphasizes leadership (Hebrews 13:17). In particular, the writer believes there are benefits when people submit to leaders. What are these benefits? There are many, but in the following, I will name two major ones:

Guidance: Lot would have died without the prayers of his uncle, Abraham. Before God destroyed Sodom and Gomorrah, He informed Abraham of what He would do. Hence, Abraham pleads with God not to destroy the righteous with the wicked in the area his nephew lived (Genesis 18:16-33). God granted Abraham's request, and Lot was warned to vacate the region.

The biblical truth is that leaders have reached a level of consecration that produces the type of authority and relationship that our sovereign God responds to. God loves all His creation, but there are moments in the scripture when one meets a particular condition established by God, and He responds. Such is the case of a man named Daniel. He was an excellent man. He stood out from among the rest. Therefore He was the only one in the Babylonian kingdom at that time who had access to interpreting dreams from God (Daniel 2). Moses was more humble than all the rest in his time. Therefore, He had access to God in a way the other Israelites did not (Numbers 12:3). Similarly, Peter, James, and John had access in a way the other disciples did not (Mark 5:37). In times past and present, God always grants authority, revelation, and power to a leader, to bring guidance to His people.

What would have happened if Joseph did not warn the people of the coming famine? Would the people not have known to save up grain for seven years? Maybe the man would have remained paralyzed had not the four friends opened a hole in the roof and laid him before Jesus (Mark 2:4)? The point is that God appoints leaders who can intervene. Sometimes a person needs intervention when a problem has become excessive, or the person does not have the education to know any better. A visionary leader can discern the things others do not see.

Promotion: God decided that some things/gifts can only be attained by connecting with others. God is satisfied to use His creation for the prosperity of others. Hence, Naaman only gets healed of his leprosy when he submits to the instruction of Elisha; David had no idea he would be king until the Prophet Samuel anointed him for the task, and Paul gave Timothy the foundation for his ministry. The Apostles Paul and Barnabas were appointed to their ministry by a council of leaders (Acts 15).

Just like Jacob knew that the birthright could only be attained through the blessing of His father Isaac or Elisha knew he had to get the mantle from Elijah, the visionary leader carries a blessing or mantle that can be imparted for a person's promotion. Some blessings can only be imputed by others.

HONOR

Honor is supposed to be a lifestyle, not an event. Honor is not limited to one's birthday, graduation from school, funerals, or wedding day. Instead, we are to live honorably and give recognition to others (Romans 13:7). When one struggles to show honor towards others; it is because that person is not humble enough to accept that someone else is more significant in a particular position, study, or field. Instead, the jealous ambition of a rebellious person attempts to steal the honor due to a great person.

Here is a remark that is true in all walks of life: "There are those whose diligence and sacrifice are greater than my own and they are worthy of my acknowledgment." The truth is that some people are more exceptional than others. Daniel, David, Deborah, Jehu, the Virgin Mary, and John the Baptist were outstanding and chosen by God for a specific purpose. One cannot pretend as if these men and women were not worthy of honor. To attempt to discredit these people would be to dishonor God Himself—it was His choice. And yes, some characters in the Bible did not follow through to the end, and none of them were flawless (E.g., King Saul). Yet, God honors King David by allowing Jesus to be called the "Son of David." All generations know about the exceptional virgin girl who gave birth to our Savior because scripture proclaimed she would be remembered (Luke 1:48). Jesus gave His cousin John the honor of being called the greatest man born of a woman (Luke 7:28). If God can honor people in scripture then His people should be able to honor others as well.

Honor is such a powerful principle that it gives access and favor to all who practice it. Esther honored the king, which caused him to extend the royal scepter to her and ultimately opened the door for her to become the queen. It was the way Ruth honored her mother-in-law, Naomi, that got her the favor of Boaz, and she became a wife (Ruth 2:11). The Roman centurion spoke with honor as he pleaded for Jesus to heal his servant, which caused Jesus to grant his request (Matthew 8:8-9).

The Apostle Paul stated, "*The elders who direct the affairs of the church well are worthy of **double honor**, especially those whose work is preaching and teaching*" (1 Timothy 5:17, emphasis mine). Without a doubt, servants of God should be worthy of honor! Even if one is not a fivefold minister or a visionary leader, all children of God are worthy of recognition because of who our Father is! We are the King's kids. Nonetheless, those servants who live at a higher level of sacrifice, some of which most people will never know, Paul says, are worthy of "double honor"—especially when handling or delivering the instruction of the Lord. This is why scripture warns people about not harming the Lord's anointed ones, for they speak on God's behalf (Psalm 105:15).

POSITION OR PERSON?

Biblically speaking, positions of authority and duty exist in heaven. What can be known from the scripture is that there are elders, angels, and even different ranks among angels in heaven (cherubim, seraphim, and arch/prince angels). Some of these angels have personal names. Gabriel was the name of the angel that visited Mary. In particular, some angels have the distinct purpose of glorifying God by delivering messages to people. At the tomb of Jesus, there were two angels whose names were not recorded, but they fulfilled the position of angels who delivered messages. Whether an angel is more personalized or not, whether a person likes or prefers different types of angels over others, angels are of consequence in that they fulfill the assignment. The same is true of earthly positions.

This is all to say that one does not have to like a person to receive the benefits from the position that person holds. Some days a person is more likable than others. And other days, you might not like the same person, but you remain committed and receive from him or her. Many people had moments in their childhood when they did not like their parents. But ideally, if your parents were good, you still respected your mother and father because they have/had the position of a parent—they still took care of you. And most likely, there were days when your parents did not find you to be the most enjoyable child.

Nonetheless, they dealt with all your destructive habits because they loved you. Why did they put up with you? Because you held the position of "child" in their life. Spouses may not like each other some days, but they still love and fulfill their husbandly and wifely duty to one another.

If you are submitted to a faithful and bonafide visionary leader, even though he is genuine, he will not be flawless (neither is the congregation member). And even if the visionary leader is not currently making mistakes, you will have some days where you may not like what your preacher says or does. It does not mean the leader has done something sinful. It simply means that it challenges your perspective and makes you uncomfortable. There were many things the disciples did not understand or like about Jesus (John 6:60, Matthew 19:25)— but they knew He was specially anointed and stayed with Him. It was not until Jesus was resurrected that they fully understood what He came to earth to do, for they were confused about Christ's purpose while He was with them (Luke 18:31-34).

If only one surgeon could remove a tumor from your body, but you did not like his hairstyle, would you refuse his expertise and die from the tumor? No, of course not. One would be a fool to refuse the doctor's help due to hairstyle. In other words, you do not have to like the doctor's hairstyle to reap the benefits of his expertise. You must show honor and civility toward the surgeon if you want his help. Otherwise, the surgeon might move on to help someone who is more appreciative.

Furthermore, when visiting a doctor for the first time, do you visit the office because you like the doctor or because of the medical expertise? Ideally, you see a doctor based on the specification of practice in the area of medicine you need. It is only when the doctor has successfully treated you that you like the physician. If the doctor cannot help you or has a terrible bedside manner, you might not think too favorably concerning that doctor. If, on the other hand, the doctor helps cure you, then you smile and give them a referral. And as you refer the doctor, you might mention the physician's sense of humor, children, style, and all those little fun side conversations you had with your doctor during consultations. First, you visit the doctor because of his or her position, and then you like the doctor's personality. Likewise, it is when you initially honor the position of the visionary leader that you begin to enjoy him as a person.

What happened with the ten lepers Jesus healed? They visit Jesus to be cleansed, but only one of the ten returns to praise Him. It was the one leper who showed the most honor, not only for the position Christ had to heal him but for the person Christ was. Jesus acknowledged that he was the only one to give thanks. No doubt this individual ex-leper honored Christ's position, but the leper liked Jesus all the more when he was healed (Luke 17:11-19).

The issue is that many Christians think they must like the visionary leader and the message first to receive anything from him. On the contrary, it is important to honor the position first. In society, at least in the United States, there is this saying: "It is a lot easier to receive the message if you like the messenger" or "You attract more bees with honey." While this is true, it is not necessarily the case in the Bible. The leadership and messages of Moses, Jeremiah, John the Baptist, and the apostles were noble even though they were hated! There is no greater message than what Jesus preached, but He was still crucified—they hated Jesus and His message! In God's kingdom, even if one does not like the messenger and the message, one must honor the position and still accept the message!

King Ahab did not like the Prophet Micaiah and his message. Therefore, he did not listen to Micaiah's prophetic warnings, which led to Ahab's death. If he would have honored Micaiah's position as a prophet, his life would have been spared

(1 Kings 22:1-28). Sometimes what people like keeps them from God's best and His protection!

What one likes changes all the time. It changes with the seasons, the era, the culture, and the political climate. What one likes when he or she is a child will change in adulthood. It is juvenile only to accept or pursue what one likes. Some things are worth pursuing even if you do not like them or it makes you uncomfortable (E.g., exercise). Sadly, in a hedonistic and emotionally charged culture, many people have resisted a good leader because the leader made them uncomfortable. In the beginning, people may not like what the fitness trainer instructs them to do; but when they reap the benefits of the fitness trainer's coaching, they are grateful.

Without a doubt, liking someone helps. But what percentage does it take to like someone? What is the approved or certifiable rate that qualifies as truly "liking" someone? Do you ever like 100% of what someone does or who someone is? Do you have to enjoy at least 50% of a person's personality for it to qualify? What about 35%? The truth is that we have to love people 100%—God commands us to love fully (John 15:12). But you do not have to like everything about people to like them still.

Even the words in someone's mouth reveal that he or she does not like everything about a person, place, or thing. People will often say, "I like…because…" And after the "because," the person may only list two or three reasons for what is liked about another person. And what is liked may only be limited to those two or three connections with said person. However, if one had more meetings with said person, one may discover that he or she only liked the person within those two or three scenarios. How often does an individual meet someone in one positive interaction and leave thinking, "I like that person!" Indeed, the individual may only like 10% of the other person's character. And yet, in one meeting, it was enough to state: "I like that person."

What I am saying is this: even if there is someone you think is annoying 95% of the time, the remaining 5% can still be enough for you to say, "I like that person." You know the annoying person is lovable and good. It just so happens that he or she annoys you. But love will compel you to be good to everyone, no matter how you feel about them. And yes, we do have to avoid dangerous people. But some good people get avoided just because someone does not like everything about that person. Be careful. You could be rejecting someone God sent to bless your life. Because people are made in the image and likeness of God, there is always something likable about a great person you may conclude is annoying. One just needs to look for the signature of God in others.

People often misjudge visionary leaders based on if they like them or not! You do not have to like everything about the visionary leader's personality for him to lead you. Is your visionary leader biblical? Is he authentically passionate about Christ? Is he anointed? If the answer is "yes," then that leader is of consequence and can bless your life if you submit to the position he has for your life. No matter how small the percentage of likability, there will be something to like so that you have positive interactions with your visionary leader. However, when dislike turns to hate, therein is rebellion, the subject we will tackle in the next couple of chapters.

Please Respect Other Leaders

It has become apparent that congregational members do not always view the other fivefold ministers associated with the visionary leader as authoritative. So when the senior/visionary leader is unavailable for a member at the moment, that member may feel that receiving ministry from the associate pastor or other ministers is insignificant. That thought could not be further from the truth.

The visionary leader of your church is a human being. He cannot always be available for all matters all the time. Moreover, the other ministers are there to love God by supporting the visionary leader in the areas he is not graced in. God chose and connected Aaron with Moses because Moses did not speak well. So Aaron became Moses' spokesman. While people may have wanted a direct conversation with Moses, sometimes they had to meet with Aaron (Exodus 4:10-31).

Furthermore, apostles tend to be direct, bold, and systematic in their presentation. If what you need is a pastoral approach that is more nurturing, and if your visionary leader is a strong and boisterous apostle, then your apostle might refer you to a pastor of your church house since the pastor is more graced for your circumstance. Yes, God has made the visionary leader the primary leader of His church house, and there are times when you need to directly meet with the visionary leader, but God also appoints other fivefold ministers along with the visionary leader. Do not insult God's choice of the other fivefold ministers who help you, including the elders, deacons, and other ministers. Always show honor.

CHAPTER TEN

REBELLION PART ONE

One of the most egregious rebellions in scripture was the defection of an angel named Lucifer. He did not want to submit to the sovereignty of Jehovah. In his foolishness, he thought he could be greater than God. Not only did Lucifer defect, but he also convinced many angels to follow him. His revolt was unsuccessful. So God hurled him out of heaven to the earth, where he is awaiting his death sentence. Meanwhile, he still attempts to rebel against God by recruiting God's people to defect from God's will.

Lucifer has become known as "Satan," which means "accuser." He accuses God and the people who follow God of falsehoods. He is a liar who thinks he can taint the name of God. The Devil is highly narcissistic, jealous, and envious. Therefore God created a place for him and the other fallen angels (Matthew 25:41).

Rebellion has always been the attempt to kill God! Rebellion is the desire to remove God of His sovereignty—no one has ever been successful! God is absolute. The sun must rise and set at the Lord's command; the winds and the waves must obey Him! There is nothing to make Him fearful; instead, He is to be feared (Proverbs 9:10). If God could be defied without repercussions, He would cease to be God. There must be a punishment for defectors; otherwise, God is not much of a God.

Earthly kings can be challenged and overthrown. An earthly king can fight back to protect his kingdom, but if the opposing king were more cunning and led a stronger army, the incumbent king would be conquered. Fortunately for us, King Jesus is not limited to being an earthly king. Even death did not hold Him. Glory be to King Jesus!

God does punish all disobedience, for no one gets to smirk and say, "I rebelled against God, and He did nothing." However, He is a God that delights in mercy (Micah 7:18). He is love. And because God is not threatened in any way, He can be slow in His punishment of the rebellious to give them time to repent. So God has prolonged His final judgment for this season that we call the dispensation of grace. Nonetheless, there are warnings or flashes of God's judgment to remind us that the rebellious and disobedient will not prosper for long. Ananias and Sapphira do not get away with lying to the Holy Spirit (Acts 5:1-11). God will allow people to go through hardships or repay evil to people, hoping they learn from their choices and repent before the final judgment (1 Corinthians 5:5). Make no mistake about it; God takes rebellion in His kingdom seriously. He will never be dethroned.

Satan is called the god of this world (2 Corinthians 4:4). He attempts to counterfeit God while on earth. And just as the Devil ruined the harmony in the Garden of Eden, the Devil wants to destroy the unity of many churches. The Devil causes divisions, gossip, factions, scandals, and many splits within a church. He knows nothing is more dangerous to his influence than a people whose God is Jehovah. The Church is the greatest establishment on the earth. It is an embassy of God's kingdom. However, when the Devil recruits Christians to cause strife in God's church, what was supposed to be a place of God's radiant glory, becomes a dim light. Church etiquette, when done right, will repel and remove rebellious people under the influence of Satan.

BIBLICAL DEFECTORS

In the Bible, many rebellious people hurt the progress of Israel. Interestingly, one of the biggest problems for God's people has always been God's people! It is always an inside job! As long as Israel was obedient to God, they won every battle. But in times of disobedience, their enemies overwhelmed them. Unfortunately, it is always the people within the church that cause a church to split. Jesus was very clear about the success of His Church. He said, "*I will build my church, and the gates of Hades will not overcome it*" (Matthew 16:18b). So long as Jesus is honored in His Church, the Church will always prosper. But when people with big egos and insecurities start a coup (just like Lucifer), there will be problems. The following are a few rebellions in the Bible that caused significant issues:

Achan (Joshua 7): God specifically told the people of Israel to save the spoils of war from Jericho for Him. However, a man named Achan did not listen to the instruction of God through His servant Joshua. He hid silver, gold, and an expensive robe under his tent. As a result, the Israelites lost their next conquest, the battle at AI, and thirty-six men died. God's favor left the people because of one man's greed.

This type of rebellious mindset causes churches to not achieve their goals. A church may need money for a community project or volunteers to maintain church grounds. However, these types of people refuse to give of their time, treasure, or talent towards it because they do not see the benefit for themselves. They have the means to help but do not. And even if they do help, it is only to make themselves look good. They are indifferent to what the leader says, even though the leader (Joshua) spoke directly on behalf of God. When people are a part of something they do not care about, they will sabotage the ones that do—36 men died at the battle of AI because of Achan's indifference.

Korah (Numbers 16): Korah was a member of Moses' council. He was supposed to be in support of Moses's leadership. However, he turned 250 people against his administration. Korah's ego consumed himself. Even though God called Moses to be the visionary leader, Korah assumed that he could have Moses' position.

This rebel insulted God by not accepting God's choice for leadership. God chose Moses to be the leader. Therefore, Moses cannot be replaced by any person unless God removes the leader. This type of person disrespects and competes with all leadership in the church. This rebel's words and actions make it appear like God made a mistake when He put the leader in charge. When God picks a leader, there is a reason for it. Korah believed himself to be more called than he was and was swallowed up by the weight of stepping into a position in which he had no authority.

Absalom (2 Samuel 15): David's son, Absalom, would stop people at the city gate who were coming to receive the counsel of King David. For four years, he recruited people by promising to help them in a way that his father could not. Absalom would have people follow him to another location beyond the gaze of David's loyal followers. He was usurping his father's leadership under the radar until it became so apparent that David heard about it. The people were slowly deceived, and Absalom convinced many Israelites to hail him as king. His rebellion gained such strength that David had to flee his city for some time.

This person is highly deceptive. No one would have thought that one of David's sons would be conspiring against him like this. This person will appear helpful and on the leader's side, but this individual is only building on someone else's platform. This person is not anointed to do it on his or her own. So a church will have Bible studies with appointed leaders, regular corporate worship times, and outreaches to the community. However, while pretending to be committed to the church, this rebel will start groups that parallel what the church is already doing to pull members away from the church. These rebels do not want to submit to what the church has already established. They are competing with the church and its leaders for influence.

People like this attend a church with an agenda outside of the church's original mission. They will only tolerate the leader in hopes of attaining a position in order to undermine the leader. They want no accountability, and they certainly do not want an authoritative leader that God has chosen to evaluate their actions.

Jezebel (1 Kings 16:29-33): Jezebel was married to King Ahab. She worshiped false gods, in particular, the pagan god Baal. As a result, of her seduction, she caused Ahab and all of Israel to worship pagan gods. King Ahab became a figurehead in Jezebel's schemes. Ahab was the puppet, and she was the puppet master pulling the strings.

These types of rebellious people look to get control of the visionary leader. They do not want to be visibly seen as the primary leader, but they do try to control everything in the church. And if things go wrong, everyone blames the visible leader instead of Jezebel, who controls things behind the scenes. These people are what you call "congregational bullies." From the congregation, they attempt to manipulate and bully the visionary leader. They make sure the leader knows what they think about the sermon, the programs, the facilities, and other leaders. God may be pleased with what the leader is doing, but this type of person ultimately tries to shape the church in his or her image. This person believes everyone should be like him or herself.

WHAT REBELS DO!

Sometimes, people attend a church and do not feel very well emotionally, physically, or spiritually. Yet regardless of how one feels, people should still show courtesy to one another. No one gets a license to belittle others because he or she is having a rough day. No one should dare insult God and steal His glory by having a bad attitude in His Church. But, sometimes, natural conditions do not represent our spiritual position. Meaning that a person may come to church with a heart that is receptive to God, even though this person feels exhausted by life. The person's heart is committed to being transparent and thereby transformed despite terrible circumstances. In other words, how can people cast their burdens on God if they pretend like the problems are not there (1 Peter 5:7)? Just because Christians occasionally have a less than cheerful appearance at church does not mean they are rebellious. They could just be having a rough time. However, when someone enters a church with a divisive motivation, there are several indicators:

Whisper: They love to gossip and bear false witness of situations they are not involved in. They want to separate people with their words (Proverbs 16:28). They especially want to cast doubt over leadership. They do not want people to be committed to the leader. The spirit controlling the defector knows that if they strike the leader or make the leader look bad, it will affect the congregation (Matthew 26:31). So, while everyone else enjoys the leader's ministry, the rebel will plant seeds of doubt concerning the leader. It sounds like this: "Well...pastor preached well, but he should have said this," or "Pastor is a good person, but I think things should have been done differently." They assume an understanding of a position God has not called or placed them.

If rebellious people have concerns about the leader or others in leadership, why do they not approach the leader first? It only makes logical sense to approach the person who can change or adapt to the concern. Jesus clearly stated that one should directly contact the person with whom he or she has an issue (Matthew 18). Christians are to look for reconciliation with one another (2 Corinthians 5:18). But that is not the motive of the rebellious! They want church members to start questioning the intent of the leader. They want people to question the leader's preaching, prayers, and leadership ability. If they are unsuccessful in bringing down the leader, they try turning members on one another.

Create confusion: These people are double talkers. One can never trust what comes out of the mouth of a deceiver. Imagine how the army of Saul felt as they were pursuing the one (David) who once led them into battle. King Saul loved David when it was convenient for him but then wanted to dispose of him as he grew in his anointing. As Saul was pursuing to murder David, he still addressed him as "son" (1 Samuel 26:17). How confusing this must have been. Saul calls David an enemy in one instance, and in another, he calls him a son. At one moment, he is soothed by the musical gifts of David and then hurling a spear at him the next!

Likewise, the congregation is confused as the rebellious person speaks positively yet negatively about the church and its leaders. Their comments always have subliminal messages attacking the integrity and durability of the church.

Intimidate: When Nehemiah was rebuilding the wall of Jerusalem, he spoke of men named Sanballat and Tobiah who were trying to intimidate him (Nehemiah 6). They did not want

Nehemiah to renovate Jerusalem even though God commissioned him. The rebellious want the leader and everyone in the church to believe that they want nothing from anybody. But the opposite is true. They crave admiration and fear from people. They have an attitude that says, "I am here to evaluate and control everyone else...no one can evaluate me... I'm just at church because I'm supposed to be."

Control: It is all about control. Satan got control over Adam and Eve in the Garden of Eden, costing them paradise. The Devil promised them something that only led to being manipulated and controlled for Satan's purposes. In the same manner, the rebellious person is ultimately a narcissist. They see the church as a playground for their self-absorbed, super-inflated egos. They want to take advantage of the kindness of Christians for their selfish ambition.

These people are deeply insecure and do not want anybody to see them for who they are. If necessary, they will project a big imposing personality to get people to submit to their false authority. And some people are fooled and will follow them in their rebellion because they appear to be confident, whereas they are deeply broken, unsure, and unfulfilled. They only feel good when people are under them.

Recruit: Rebellious people never have the stamina to stand on their own. They always need to recruit innocent or naive people into their schemes. Satan recruited angels to go against God; Korah recruited 250 people to go against Moses; Absalom convinced a large majority of Israelites to go against David; Jezebel controlled and enticed King Ahab to turn Israel over to false idols. However, God's truly anointed man or woman has the capacity and strength to stand alone, even if no one follows.

Jeremiah had to stand alone as Israel insulted him! Elijah was the only one willing to challenge the prophets of Baal, and he stood alone by the brook as God miraculously took care of him. The Apostle Paul had to stand alone on the Areopagus as he told the men of Athens who the real God was (Acts 17:22). Jesus was alone on the cross as the world rejected Him. Even God, the Father, had forsaken Him (Matthew 27:46). These leaders could accomplish their tasks because God was backing them! They did not need to gossip, intimidate, slander, or do anything the rebellious do to recruit people.

It is obvious who the rebellious people are. They are forever recruiting people into their slanderous, gossiping, conniving, and self-absorbed scheme. The rebellious will find a false prophet, minister, or spiritual person that claims to be an authority but is just as rebellious as them to affirm their defection. Saul connected with the witch of Endor; Judas conspired with the chief priest against Jesus, and Saul of Tarsus attained permission from the chief priest to attack Christians. They will say, "Another pastor/elder agrees with me...that's why I am doing it." But God is not with them.

Liars: As a last resort, when their plans to secretly and slowly dismantle a church and its leader have failed, they will lie (Proverbs 19:9). This is when the rebellious are at their lowest. Once they are about to be discovered for what they have done secretly, they will conjure up false narratives as they leave the church. God was about to expose them publicly, so they dismissed themselves while telling lies. And as they go, they tend to claim that someone is after or attacking them, yet no one is chasing them. And the congregation feels relief from their departure. But what is chasing them is their overwhelming guilt and shame for all the dishonor they sowed! *"Do not be deceived: God cannot be mocked. A man reaps what he sows"* (Galatians 6:7).

WHY DO THEY BECOME REBELS?

Anxiousness: For some reason, they are very insecure people. Anxiousness will always make you doubtful and suspicious of others. When one fears the unknown, one becomes anxious. They will claim to not fit into any system because they are too brilliant or different. The truth is that they could belong but choose not to.

God commands that we love our neighbor as ourselves (Mark 12:31). Scripture teaches that we cannot say we love God if we do not love people (1 John 4:20). Love requires trust. And this is the struggle of every rebellious person. They sabotage what could have been good relationships because of their trust issues.

Competitiveness: They believe they must prove themselves to God and others. They have not learned to be content in the position or ministry God has given. They will not openly admit it, but they regularly feel insignificant. And believe that they must always be in the top and most recognized position or at least in control of the one that is.

One needs to understand that God has already given people their assignments before birth. Jeremiah was destined to be a prophet. If he had tried to be a musician, soldier, cook, or king, he would have missed the mark (Jeremiah 1:5). All Jeremiah had to do was continue to maximize and be promoted in the sphere of influence God had given him as a prophet—and he did!

Sadly, rebellious people constantly compete for what they think is the best or most prominent position. They will try to be apostles, although they are not apostles. They will try to take over the worship team even though they are not the worship director. Even if they have not been appointed and do not have the title, they will carry themselves as if they do. They would be filled with joy if they accepted the calling God has given them, but the Devil steals their joy and makes them a competitor.

Reprobate mind: When a person refuses to believe the truth and continues to stand in the way of God's plan, the Lord will eventually turn them over to a reprobate mind. After God has given people plenty of warnings, and they still refuse, He allows a rebellious person to believe the lie. The Apostle Paul mentions this as he talks about why wicked people die, saying, "*They perish because they refused to love the truth and so be saved. For this reason, God sends them a powerful delusion so that they will believe the lie and so that all will be condemned who have not believed the truth but have delighted in wickedness*" (2 Thessalonians 2:10-12).

The startling truth about God is that He is merciful, yet because He knows all things, when a person rejects the truth for too long, that person's conscience becomes seared, and He stops warning them—judgment takes place. After a while, God flooded the entire earth. He set ablaze Sodom and Gomorrah, hardened the pharaoh's heart so that he could not change his course toward devastation, and shut the door to the five foolish virgins.

Jesus did not stop Judas from betraying Him. Why? He knew Judas was not going to change. God turned him over to a reprobate mind, and Christ told him to do it quickly (John 13:27). This is why some people become rebels. They have lived in such defiance of the will of God for so long that God has given them over to their wicked desire. Unfortunately, they did not realize that what they desired would lead them to their doom—such is the case of Judas' terrible end. God will get His glory out of people one way or another. Even though Judas rebelled, he still served God's purpose in getting Christ to the cross and serving as a warning to us.

THE CHURCH IS NOT A DEMOCRACY

This heading may come as a surprise to some, but it is indeed the truth. While many, including myself, think democracy is the best we can do with our earthly governments, Jesus is the King. Christianity exists within a monarchy, not a democracy. Jesus is the ruler, and what He says becomes law. Therefore, as Christians, we do our best to follow earthly governments so long as they do not impede our kingdom's citizenship.

Hence one of the problems within the Church is that people think every matter requires a vote. Whereas in God's kingdom, voting is not required. The Prophet Samuel was at one time God's appointed man over Israel. Not everyone agreed with Samuel, even though he spoke on behalf of God. And in their disapproval of him, they did not realize they were disagreeing with the God that supported Samuel (1 Samuel 8:6-7). There is great counsel among other believers (Proverbs 11:14). Even Moses had his father-in-law that gave him counsel. But ultimately, God places one person in charge to delegate His will. As the saying goes, "Anything with two heads is a monster or a deformity." And monstrous things have happened in God's house when a church is perceived as a democracy instead of a monarchy. It was never God's intention for the entire congregation to take on the burden of leadership by voting for everything. I explained this in more detail in my book called *Fivefold Ministry: Access Granted:*

> *The Fivefold is an authoritative and Biblical model of doing church. It's not like the congregationalist model, where regardless of the maturity level, each member gets a vote. No, that model often empowers the Judas of your congregation to vote, and we all know that Judas votes for his selfish ambitions. Moreover, when the whole congregation of Israel voted for or against Jesus to die, they*

chose Barrabas over Jesus (John 18:38-40). I am not saying a congregation cannot be trusted, it's just wrong to assume or place the burden of leadership on the entire congregation and make them accountable before a holy God. Not everyone is at that place of leadership. There should be a true leader that willingly stands out and makes the tough decisions, so the rest can live in freedom.

Some people criticize Fivefold ministry because of its authoritative sense of the visionary leader—for they make the final decision. But the reality is, whenever the whole congregation gets a vote on what God wants the church to do, it automatically produces division or a schism. Because one half of the church votes "yes" and the other half votes "no." So now the church breaks out into factions, just like the divide between republicans and democrats in the United States, and nothing gets done in the church. Or if they do not break out into factions, then they become despondent to the mission of the church, and become passive voters because they know their vote can be cancelled out if they are in the minority.

Furthermore, the truth of the matter is that there is always one person or a small group running the entire church even if it appears to be a congregational vote. There is always the person that has given the most money, has the most family members at the church, appears to be the most talented and anointed, or has been at the church the longest that tries to have the biggest voice and turn people's votes. As much as we try to deny it, if you have been involved in church leadership for a little while, you know there is always a single visionary leadership present through an individual or a small group of affluent people.

Hence, the Fivefold just points out the obvious...that the church does need a visionary leader to make final decisions if the church wants to get everything done. God does send a visionary like Abraham, Moses, Deborah, David, Solomon, John the Baptist, Paul, Peter, and the like, to galvanize people towards the will of God. The visionary Fivefold leader does need the wise council of other Fivefold ministers, elders, etc., it's just that it should not come from everybody. It should be wise council assisting the visionary leader to make godly decisions, like Jonathan was to David. (125-126)

The kingdom of God and the King's Church is not to be run like a democracy, but its visible leader is not to be a tyrant either. If a person is a real visionary leader, that person will lead with the grace and boldness that is representative of the King. And the Church will make kingdom advancements.

THE VISIONARY LEADER IS NOT A DICTATOR

For the sake of clarity, the visionary leader is not a dictator. There are various planes or tiers of leadership within the church and different workers of ministries. God has entrusted the overall mission of a particular church to a visionary leader. And the visionary leader is supposed to keep oversight so that all things are decent and in order (1 Corinthians 14:40). However, the visionary leader cannot and should not be involved in all the details. In others words, there will be freedom within delegation for people within a church to operate with their gifts. David had the vision for the temple, but others built it (1 Chronicles 28:2-7)! The visionary leader will need to give freedom to other leaders and ministry workers in the congregation to operate with their talents and gifts to accomplish what God desires.

The visionary leader will have a vision of what God wants to do at a church house. If one does not share the vision, that person should not be there. There is another church that person should submit to. But as a result of the shared vision, the visionary leader will delegate as the Lord leads him, and everyone will enjoy victory together. As the Bible states,

Even so the body is not made up of one part but of many.
Now if the foot should say, 'Because I am not a hand, I do not belong to the body,' it would not for that reason stop being part of the body. And if the ear should say, 'Because I am not an eye, I do not belong to the body,' it would not for that reason stop being part of the body. If the whole body were an eye, where would the sense of hearing be? If the whole body were an ear, where would the sense of smell be? But in fact God has placed the parts in the body, every one of them, just as he wanted them to be. If they were all one part, where would the body be? As it is, there are many parts, but one body. (1 Corinthians 12:14-20)

As has been alluded to in this chapter, the rebellious struggle to do the part God has assigned to them. They want control over others even if God has not called them to lead. Hence, no matter what the true leader does, they will assume the worst of the leader. The rebellious, much like Satan, always accuse leaders of being a dictator. King Ahab, who was rebellious, called Elijah a "troublemaker" even though Elijah was a true leader (1 Kings 18:17). While there are false leaders that need to step down, not every authoritative leader is a dictator. Some people are just rebellious and never want to be held accountable.

YOUR RESPONSE TO REBELLION
IN THE CHURCH

Dear reader, what the enemy wants to do through a rebellious person is create a church environment that is toxic and exhaustive. The enemy's goal is to make the environment so harsh that people want to leave. During a coup, people left churches not because the leaders were proven false but because the climate became too burdensome. It is as if the people say, "I love the church's mission, the people, and the leadership, but the tension has become too difficult for my family and me to deal with…I think I will start looking for a new church."

Have you ever been in a room where someone was arguing? Was it a comfortable experience? This is the toxic environment the Devil wants to produce in your church. Do not let it happen! Whenever a rebellious person gives you a phone call, text message, email, or meets you for lunch or in the corner somewhere, and begins to demonstrate any of the rebellious traits mentioned in this chapter, the following is what you can do:

Stop the gossip: If people have a problem with the leader, are looking for a ministry position, or want to see a new ministry launched within the church, nicely tell them to speak to leadership. If they are rebellious, they will leverage your conversation and claim you as a participant in their unsanctioned endeavors.

Therefore, if you do not have a leadership/ministry position to help with their complaint, then you cannot help them. If they want help, they should have no problem submitting to leadership by speaking with them. Even if they say that leadership told them "no" or has not gotten back to their formal request, there might be a reason for that! Just refer them to leadership again and change the conversation.

Do not spread the gossip: You must not walk around your church with your guard up, as if everyone is a potential threat. Church members are your brothers and sisters in Christ. We must be vulnerable with one another. Yet, in innocence, you may have entertained someone's gossip, thinking it was a genuine conversation. Therefore, makes sure not to spread it to other people.

Sometimes when a person hears something negative, they look to speak to someone they are comfortable with. And then it spreads from one person to the next. Although each person's original intent was to solve the problem, it creates tension in the congregation. Because as the gossip spreads, specific points get lost or exaggerated. Now congregants who had nothing to do with the original issue begin to criticize one another because of misinformation. People break into factions and begin to take sides, and what was once a unified church body becomes divided—precisely what the Devil wanted to accomplish. Again, this will exhaust the community of faith. Please seek out a designated leader who can solve the problem.

Tell leadership immediately: A leader should not be kept in the dark about rebellion in the church. If someone is secretly deceiving people out of the church, speaking negatively about leadership and the like, the visionary leader needs to know about it. Jonathan informed David of King Saul's plots against him (1 Samuel 19:1-3). And Jesus knew that Judas was going to betray Him. Rebellion is like cancer or mold. The sooner you stop it, the less damage it causes.

The next chapter will address excommunication as an option for dealing with rebellion.

Pray: God knows what to do. So make sure you include God. Conflict is very stressful. Do not let the enemy make you anxious. Rebellious people will pressure you to defect and follow in their traitorous behavior—do not be bullied. They will manipulate scripture and say that God is telling you to join them in their coup or to leave. Be strong.

Lastly, know that everything is well. Do not let the Devil fog your mind. If you know that the people are sincere and the leaders genuinely love Jesus, if your life has been changed, do not let rebellious people make you think differently. A real visionary leader (pastor, apostle, and others) will love you. The leader cares about your success. You know you have grown deeper in your devotion and relationship with Christ due to your church. Do not be deceived now.

Just think about it! Would you want to be like the rebellious person conspiring against your church? The rebellious are jealous, envious, insecure, and frustrated. They seem charming and capable, but underneath, they are discontent. A truly secure person does not have to use others as a stepping stool to attain success. A person of great character does not have to belittle others to feel validated. But that is what the rebellious do. And to follow them in their dissension would make you just like them. Go directly through the proper leadership channels of your church so it can be dealt with immediately. Do not let a Jezebel, Absalom, Korah, or any divisive person bully you into becoming a lesser version of yourself.

CHAPTER ELEVEN

REBELLION PART TWO

Sometimes what people call controlling is actually leading. God chooses a visionary leader who can accurately understand His heart or will without tampering with it. Should a visionary leader's conscience become seared, and he loses his ability to correctly discern and employ God's will, then God removes that leader as He did King Saul. Let us look at a few biblical instances where God told His leaders not to embrace or accept certain people for ministry.

1 Samuel 16:6-7: "...*Samuel saw Eliab and thought, 'Surely the Lord's anointed stands here before the Lord.' But the Lord said to Samuel, 'Do not consider his appearance or his height, for I have rejected him. The Lord does not look at the things people look at. People look at the outward appearance, but the Lord looks at the heart.'*"

It may have "appeared" like Eliab would have made a good king, but appearances can be deceiving—his heart was not right. Some people have degrees of education, physical stature, great personality, and resources, but they are not fit for leadership. They have never developed the right maturity or were never called to leadership.

Judges 7:4: "*But the Lord said to Gideon, 'There are still too many men. Take them down to the water, and I will thin them out for you there. If I say, 'This one shall go with you,' he shall go; but if I say, 'This one shall not go with you,' he shall not go.*"

God decided to limit the number of fighting men Gideon would need for war. In so doing, God does not want everybody for every assignment. It is not just about availability; it is about responsibility. In other words, who has God chosen for the task? Otherwise, extra people may be a distraction instead of a help.

Acts 8:20-23: "*Peter answered: 'May your money perish with you, because you thought you could buy the gift of God with money! You have no part or share in this ministry, because your heart is not right before God. Repent of this wickedness and pray to the Lord in the hope that he may forgive you for having such a thought in your heart. For I see that you are full of bitterness and captive to sin.'*"

A man named Simon, who practiced sorcery, wanted to pay for the power of the Holy Spirit. He was wrong for thinking the Holy Spirit could be bought. And upon evaluating his character, the Apostle Peter knew he was not fit for ministry.

Notice that God did not approve of these people in the above-mentioned scriptures. But God spoke through His visionary leaders to deny these unauthorized people. What if Samuel had ignored God and anointed Eliab king? What if Gideon decided to keep all the men for the war? What if Peter had taken money from Simon in exchange for power? These visionary leaders would have been in direct defiance and rebellion against God.

It may seem logical to anoint a man who looks like a king, to take money offered, and to get as many volunteers for war as possible, but if God says "no," there is a reason. This is not just a matter of maturity. It is a matter of God gifting and anointing a person as a visionary leader who can hear and see what others do not.

Rebellious people do not understand, or they do not want to embrace the leader God has chosen. So they resist and come against the leader, not accepting that God was speaking through His chosen vessel. No matter how qualified people might think they are, Samuel, Gideon, Peter, and other visionary leaders whom the Holy Spirit empowers, are given the arduous task of keeping the body of Christ accountable. Sometimes the leader has to tell certain people they are not fit for particular ministries. But a rebellious person will claim the visionary leader is a "cult leader" or "controlling" when all the leader is doing is fulfilling his role by speaking or enacting what the King states.

Even the apostles of the New Testament talked about people who were trying to lead others, and they were not "authorized" by their council (Acts 15:24). There are Christians who not only display maturity but are called to a ministerial office (fivefold), in which they guard the integrity of the ministry. They are given authority and wisdom to approve what is of God and not. That is why people would come to Moses, David, and Deborah to judge matters on behalf of God. And in the New Testament, it was primarily the apostles and other elders that made final decisions on behalf of God's Church. Every Christian has the Holy Spirit, but not all have been given the gifts or the office of visionary leadership.

Nonetheless, a rebellious person believes no one should be an authority over them. They will say, "Only God can tell me what to do." Yet, God is telling them what to do through His vessel.

THE DIFFERENCE BETWEEN CONTROLLING AND LEADING

Controlling is when the Israelites are told by the pharaoh they cannot worship (Exodus 10:3-5), but leading is when the Israelites are instructed on the right way of worship. (I.e., they were not supposed to worship God through a golden calf.)

Controlling is when one is told not to eat. However, leading is when the Israelites were told to only take a certain amount of food for the day (Exodus 16:19). In other words, a visionary leader is meant to lead or guide you within the sphere they have been given authority.

Imagine a soccer coach trying to train his team on the game's rules. Everyone accepts that the game being taught is soccer, and the coach is the leader. However, one rebellious player wants to pick up the soccer ball with his hands and run it into the goal like an American football player. Also, during practice, the rebellious player begins physically tackling people to the ground. He even tried to change the coach's playbook claiming that he had better strategies. So the coach stops practice and explains to the rebellious player that this is not how the game of soccer is played. After several warnings, the rebellious player continues to not follow the coach's instructions.

Should the coach change the rules for this one rebellious player? The coach is qualified by his training, experience, and credentials to be the coach—should the coach relinquish his authority? Indeed, the coach is not wrong for wanting his players to submit to his authority. He is the one in charge. Moreover, soccer is played around the globe! There are rules and guidelines that the world accepts about the game of soccer which cannot be altered. Even the most inexperienced person knows that one should not use his or her hands to score while playing soccer! Hence, the coach tells the rebellious player to leave the field and pursue American football.

This is precisely what rebellious people do in churches. They try to change the structure and order for themselves. Even if the church had existed before they arrived, they believe their presence warrants everyone's conformity. Every church's primary purpose is to glorify God through the Son, and God gives each church a different plan for achieving that. But rebellious people believe each church should follow their dogma or "playbook." As a result, they have no respect for the church or its leaders. And they will try to recruit you out of your church to follow them in their foolishness. Never allow a rebellious person to change your perspective of your church or its leaders.

A visionary leader will not force or manipulate you spiritually, physically, or emotionally—that is what tyrants like the pharaoh, Jezebel, Absalom, or the example of the rebellious soccer player does. But the leader will tell you what God desires.

STRUGGLING TO SUBMIT?

There are legitimate reasons why some people feel like they are disconnected from their church and its leaders. In the following are four reasons you may not be connecting with your church and its leader's guidance.

Ignorance: There is nothing wrong with your church. It is a biblical church. However, you may not be at the church God has called you to. Perhaps in ignorance, you chose your church out of convenience (proximity to your house, children's programs, and the like). And you feel uncomfortable because God is telling you, "You're not where you're supposed to be!"

Growth: You may have outgrown your church (you need different training). Your next level requires new relationships. It is not that your relationships at your current church are wrong, and they can remain intact in some form. Yet, God is telling you to move on.

These initial reasons should not cause one to complain and cause strife at a church. Instead, one should be grateful for the growth and revelation received from said church. Let the leaders discern with you the next step in your life. In other words, let them know God is calling you elsewhere. Do not speak in a manner that poisons the minds of what others think about the church because of your absence. God could have had you there for a season to learn things, but it is still a good church. Just because a church is not growing one person does not mean it is not growing others. So make sure to leave with honor and not belittle a church that God supports.

Lukewarm: You may not be making the most of the ministry and relationships at your church. So naturally, you feel disconnected. You sign up for ministries, small groups, and counseling sessions but never follow through. Your church attendance is lacking. And you are afraid to get out of your comfort zone and participate. Hence, you run the risk of feeling out of place, but you need to get in position and participate. Accept the challenge to become more at your church. God wants you involved.

Rebellion: You may be assaulting the church by being rebellious because you never want to submit to any authority. When you are rebellious, you may appear to be submissive to leadership, but it will only be on the surface to attain what you want—which is control. You may accuse the leaders of being controlling, but you are the controlling one, hiding under the guise of wanting to "help" leadership. You may talk badly about leaders and the church in hopes of gaining influence over people. You may appear charming from the outside but you are secretly trying to plant seeds of doubt to get others to follow you instead of the leader. In so doing, you will never feel connected to the church or the leadership because you are not genuinely vulnerable and are continuously hiding your true self and agenda.

These are just a few reasons people may feel disconnected from their church. It often has to do with a lack of submission to the process. And while there are legitimate reasons for leaving a church, rebellion is never the right way.

EXCOMMUNICATION

Imagine a shepherd inviting a wolf into the sheep pen instead of running the wolf away. Imagine a husband not willing to protect his family from intruders. Or a security guard who allows dangerous people to enter an establishment. Naturally, one would conclude that the people in these positions are negligent. They either do not care enough about their job or the people to protect them. In the same way, one is not a real leader if he or she is not prepared to excommunicate.

There is a severe caution for those that do not protect God's house. Eli, the priest, had rebellious sons who were making sexual advancements on the women at the tabernacle and taking more from the offerings than they should. Eli knew this and refused to stop his boys (1 Samuel 2:12-36). Therefore, God cursed his family line. Of course, as New Testament believers, we are under the dispensation of grace. Nevertheless, the warning is piercing. That is why the Bible informs us that not many should be teachers because the judgment will be more strict (James 3:1). If one is to be a visionary leader of God's flock, one should be committed to protecting the flock by removing the rebellious people who cause division.

The Bible makes provision for excommunication. Paul instructs that the Church mark or identify those that cause division in the church (Romans 16:17-18). He taught that the Church is to warn divisive people twice and, if they continue in rebellion, to have no fellowship with them (Titus 3:9-11).

Again, Paul said to get an immoral and rebellious person out of the church and turn that person over to Satan (1 Corinthians 5:5). Jesus said if a person is at fault, first speak to that person personally. If the person does not repent, talk to the offender with witnesses present. And then, if the individual still does not repent, let the church (leadership) deal with it. And if they do not listen to the church, Jesus said to treat that one like a pagan or tax collector, which meant to have nothing to do with them (Matthew 18:15-17). Why would Jesus say something like this? Because God Himself did not put up with rebellion. He cast Satan out of heaven when he rebelled against God.

As stated in the previous chapter, let leadership know when someone is trying to use you to scheme against leaders, create cliques and break up the general harmony of the church. If your church has blessed you, do not tolerate such cancerous people. Truthfully, too many people have entertained gossip about their spiritual leader in an attempt to be polite. Sometimes we engage in gossip, but it is harmful. Why would anybody join a church or any organization and then persistently talk badly about its leaders and members? Perhaps that person is only there with an assignment from the Devil, and they want an audience with you. True leaders will practice excommunication to protect God's people. It is necessary and biblical.

REPENTANCE FOR THE REBELLIOUS

Often, it is hard for the rebellious to confess and repent of their divisive ways. Pride overtakes the rebellious so much that they often go to the bitter end with a rebellious heart and are unapologetic for the chaos they cause. They are self-proclaimed heroes. They feel like martyrs for a cause God is not supporting. In their minds, the Devil has deceived them into believing they are correct and everyone else is wrong. Unfortunately, the rebellious often die in their sin. Rebellious people like Judas,

Korah, Achan, Jezebel, and Absalom die horrible deaths. Even the chief of all rebellion (Satan) will come to a painful end (Revelation 20:10).

If you have practiced rebellion or been complacent with acts of rebellion (such as listening to gossip, allowing the rebellious person to recruit you, and the like), I want you to know that Jesus died, so you did not have to. Judas decided to take his own life on a tree because he did not understand that it would be Christ's death on a tree that would save him (Acts 5:30)! Do not let your rebellion kill you. Christ loves the world. You are no different from the rest who have sinned and fallen short of what God designed for us all. If these couple of chapters on rebellion were an eye-opener for you. And you realize the areas you have practiced rebellion; please deal with it. Confess and repent. You may have to make some phone calls and makes amends where necessary. Christ's sacrifice is enough to compensate for your sin and redeem the time. Trust in Him.

CHAPTER TWELVE

ADVISING THE VISIONARY LEADER

Having made it to the concluding chapter of this book, I know there is more that could have been discussed. Church Etiquette is a broad topic that could be explored in many books. What remains foundational and true is that there will always be a leader. Wherever there is an organization, direction and correction are required. Someone will fill the void of leadership formally or informally. At the base of all protocol or etiquette, is a leader who established it, and leaders that maintain it. Father Abraham established what it meant to be in a relationship with God, and we all maintain it. And when people have this belief, their behavior (etiquette) will follow their belief. But when their behavior does not, God sends a leader to bring correction (2 Samuel 12:1-14).

This book has been an attempt to point to the truth—a visionary leader is always necessary. And now, at the end of this matter, I want to turn my focus and personally speak to current or future visionary leaders and leaders in general.

What I write in the following will be a raw and honest approach. If it comes across as disappointing in tone, that is not the goal. The Church has always been a triumph, but some subjects must be addressed. For there are many issues that happen within churches that many do not know about. Partially because good leaders try to keep the drama away from the people as much as possible, and while some of what I say may come across as a shock for innocent church members who are not aware of such trials in church, it will simultaneously bring much-needed relief to leaders who do not know that all true leaders go through such hardships.

There is a tangible misery to ministry. The leader works very hard to keep the peace at the expense of his or her health. Sometimes, people do not know that the visionary leader is on the verge of insanity for the sake of the people. David had to pretend like he was insane so no one would recognize and kill him (1 Samuel 21). The Apostle Paul was called insane (Acts 26:24) and claimed to have "lost his mind" for the sake of Christ (2 Corinthians 5:13). Jesus was called insane by His own family (Mark 3:21).

Why are they on the edge of insanity? Because the visionary leader lives between two worlds: the spiritual and the natural world. They are constantly dealing with angels and demons. Christians tend to believe they are living in the same tension as the visionary leader, but I assure you they are not. They may deal with angels and demons but not at the same intensity. The archer who shoots the arrow at a distance is still in a battle, but not like the one charging forth into bloody conflict! There is a battle the visionary leader has to endure that nobody else understands.

The best way to explain it is when Jesus was in the Garden of Gethsemane. There was a cup of suffering that only He could partake of. The intensity was so great that His sweat was like drops of blood (Luke 22:44). The visionary leader has the honor and displeasure of dealing with unique challenges as Jesus did. So I am going to bring you behind the scenes of what your pastor or fivefold ministers wrestle with. And for you leaders, I pray this chapter will remind you that you are God's choice for leadership. Just keep building for God.

YOU WILL EXPERIENCE BETRAYAL

Dear leader, betrayal is imminent. If it has not happened yet, it will happen. It does not mean you are a terrible leader. It is just part of the process of leadership! It simply means that there are negative people around you or people that misunderstand you. Although your intentions are pure, noble, and clear; although you are anointed, gifted, genuine, and compelling; some people are determined to misunderstand you. While what you seek as a leader is the good of those you lead, at times, those in your camp betray you.

As the leader, there is always a gap between you and the people—they are following you because of your difference and not your sameness! There must be a gap and difference between you and the people; otherwise, you cannot lead them anywhere. A toddler cannot parent another toddler. An illiterate person cannot teach another person to be literate. In other words, as the leader, you are anointed, gifted, and mature enough to help people reach their potential. And because you are ahead of everyone else in terms of foresight and insight for the common good, sometimes people cannot keep up with the direction or pace you are leading people.

For example, I used to jog with a US Marine who was a better jogger than me. We would run two or eight miles each outing at an incredible pace. Some friends who would see us running would say that our jogging pace was more like a sprint! And I was always behind him, struggling to keep up. He was the lead runner, and I was tasked with keeping up with his excellence. Sometimes we would get others to jog with us, and what began with excitement and enjoyment ended with them becoming annoyed with the pace and distance my Marine friend would set. As a result, they would stop running, turn around and go home.

I was never upset with the pace my friend would set. I needed his leadership to make me healthier and a better runner. When I would begin to slow down, he would run back towards me, place his hand on my back, and push me to keep running while yelling, "Oorah!" Because of his leadership in fitness, I became a better runner, and today, I live a healthier lifestyle. That is what leadership can do for a person when a good leader is accepted.

The same is true for the Christian leader. Some people start the "jog" with you but cannot keep the pace you set as the leader. They may have joined your church because of some personal or superficial reason. They may have liked a few sermons, the style of service, the programs, or the mission statements. However, they did not realize the stamina and humility it would take to be under your leadership once they joined. Some will be humble enough to depart nicely while honoring your position, and some will adjust and grow from your leadership.

In contrast, because of pride and embarrassment, others will make an excuse, claim they are quitting, or start fighting against you because you are a terrible leader. They may have even made promises to you while claiming they were committed and willing to participate—in their initial excitement, they overstated and overestimated their ability. And before they are exposed as inadequate, they blame you for their inability. Hence, they betray you because they do not want to admit they cannot keep up. Or they try to bring you to a lower level and compete with you, whereas they should be learning from you.

Throughout the Bible, many leaders were betrayed by people they were leading or trusting. Cain should have learned from Able, but instead, he killed him. Saul should have easily transferred power to David, but he fought him. Judas should have submitted to Jesus, but he betrayed Him. One would think all of Israel would have respected Moses, but they rejected his leadership the whole time in the wilderness. It is not always the case that a church or any organization fails because of its leader. Sometimes it is just bad followers. An entire generation of Israelites died in the wilderness, but Moses was not a bad leader. Jesus' followers deserted Him, but Jesus was not a bad leader.

Do not take betrayal personally and get bitter—instead, you must get tougher! If you cannot handle betrayal, you are not fit for leadership. Did God leave you? Did God make a mistake when He chose you? The answer is "no." Therefore you must keep leading with the grace given to you while understanding that your job as a leader has always been to elevate or eliminate.

Your choices as a leader will naturally separate and expose people for who they are! Peter gets exposed as a coward who denies knowing Jesus but ultimately gets elevated and becomes the great Apostle Peter! On the contrary, Judas gets exposed as greedy and eliminates himself by dying a sad death. As a result of being around Jesus, one man was elevated, and the other eliminated. Like Jesus, your presence as a leader causes some to rise and others to fall. And you are not doing this intentionally; it is the nature of leadership. Therefore, you cannot be surprised when your leadership attracts enemies.

Always remember this, three months is a season! If, after three months, some people are still guarded and questioning your intentions, although you are noble, they are not following you. These people are spying on you! Before long, the Devil will give them a false reason to hate you. If you constantly try to prove to them that you are trustworthy, just stop! They do not and will not trust you. And they likely have a history of being this way with many leaders. Unless God tells you otherwise, the season is done after three months! Judas, Korah, and Jezebel are always determined to disagree with you no matter what you do. Move on. Stay focused. You are wanted. You are helpful. You are a blessing.

YOU WILL BE HATED

Many times as Jesus was teaching and performing miracles, there would be religious people listening who despised Him. Among His disciples, there was Judas, who misunderstood and detested Jesus. Pharisees would send insurgents among His disciples to trap and manipulate His words. As Jesus spoke to crowds, He would see some people who looked at Him with apathy and insincerity. He had to preach to people He knew would betray Him. And some wanted Him dead before He went to the cross. Jesus said that the world hated Him. Likewise, His followers will also be hated (John 15:18).

As a visionary leader, you will sometimes preach to people in the congregation who despise you. Who scoff at your ideas and whisper to others about what they perceive as your incompetence. You will visit, pray for, give to, equip people for ministry, and love people who will not love you back. Some will assume you are a false teacher, cult leader, uninspired, ignorant, and not called by God. Others will come against you as if they are doing God a favor (John 16:2). You will be treated like your Savior Jesus, who washed the feet of people who would betray Him. It is your greatest privilege to be like Him and your greatest pain.

Jesus healed lepers, a crippled arm, a woman with an issue of blood, and raised His friend Lazarus who was dead. He miraculously fed thousands of people and supernaturally provided wine for a wedding. He opened the eyes of the blind, gave hearing to the deaf, cast out demons, provided money to pay for someone's taxes, and enlightened darkened minds. One would think that someone would have come to Jesus' defense when He was falsely accused. Somebody should have been willing to stand up for Jesus. Instead, by the shouts of "crucify Him," He was sent to the cross. Regardless of all the good He did, no one came to His defense and said, "Stop, this is a good man...do not crucify Him!"

This same thing has or will happen to you as a leader. By God's grace, I have seen God work miracles through me. I have laid my hands on people and have seen feet, backs, knees, fingers, shoulders, respiratory issues, and the like be healed; I have given people money, opportunities, and positions in ministry; I have mourned with people over their family crisis, drove miles to be with people, prayed for others several times, and these same people walked away telling people false narratives of conversations or interactions they had with me. I have seen people who appeared to be full-grown adults with children or grandchildren revert to the adolescent antics of lying, gossiping, and playing the popularity game by attempting to destroy the reputation of a good leader.

King David had this same heartache as he recalls false witnesses issuing false claims:

Ruthless witnesses come forward; they question me on things I know nothing about. They repay me evil for good and leave me like one bereaved. Yet when they were ill, I put on sackcloth and humbled myself with fasting. When my prayers returned to me unanswered, I went about mourning as though for my friend or brother. I bowed my head in grief as though weeping for my mother. But when I stumbled, they gathered in glee; assailants gathered against me without my knowledge. They slandered me without ceasing. Like the ungodly they maliciously mocked; they gnashed their teeth at me. (Psalm 35:11-16)

David is clearly in pain as he speaks about these false witnesses betraying him. David had fasted and prayed for them, but they returned evil for his good. And the same will happen to you as a leader. You have or will care for people that will not appreciate you. As the leader, you will have to accept that some people lie about your character, which will cause other people who hear the gossip to distrust or even depart from you. Because of false testimony, some people will treat you like a curse instead of a blessing. You will have to get comfortable with people not knowing your side of the story but rejoicing that God defends you (Psalm 27:2-3).

Make no mistake about it, when someone attempts to assassinate your character with false testimonies, that person is hateful (Proverbs 26:28). They do not just dislike you. But instead, they are hatefully attempting to make you seem evil. Jesus should have never been compared to Barrabas. Jesus was innocent, and Barrabas was guilty. But the people chose Barrabas over Jesus and made Jesus seem like a monster.

Should you quit when this level of hatred happens to you as the leader? No! Quitting is what the Devil hopes you will do. God called you. God chose you even though some people will not. God made you the leader because you can handle the conflict. Do not believe the lie that no one has ever experienced as much hatred as you. As the scripture states, "...*do not be surprised at the fiery ordeal that has come on you to test you, as though something strange were happening to you. But rejoice inasmuch as you participate in the sufferings of Christ, so that you may be overjoyed when his glory is revealed. If you are insulted because of the name of Christ, you are blessed, for the Spirit of glory and of God rests on you*" (1 Peter 4:12-14).

DO NOT LIVE BY PEOPLE'S EXPECTATIONS

I became a senior pastor when I was 23 years old. It was a learning experience. And there was one lady who had all these expectations of me that were not necessary. I remember talking to an experienced pastor about the situation, who gave me advice that I have never forgotten. He said, "Brian, when you're in leadership, it is always best to make decisions based on your calling, gifts, and ability. You are there to lead them, not the other way around. Stretching yourself beyond your calling will not be sustainable. You'll get tired and be good for no one."

Dear leader, one of the things I have come to embrace throughout my years of ministry is that I will never be good enough for people. Some will say the sermon is too short or too long; others will claim to be uncomfortable with the prophetic, the casting out of demons, and miracles in general. Still, others will complain that you missed their phone call, walked past them after service without saying "hello," you lack programs, or they do not like your clothing and hairstyle. Some will claim you are holding them back, whereas the Holy Spirit and qualified leaders know they are not ready for a particular ministry. The list goes on and on. But those that are with you will be with you. Accept that you cannot be everything everyone wants, but you can be exactly what God wants. The faster you learn this lesson, the freer your ministry will be.

Some people will come and go! Truly some will leave and curse your name. However, you are the one who always stays. Therefore, ensure the church's standards and protocol are biblical and match how God anointed you. Never change for seasonal people. Always remember that God called you for a reason. Your training, experience, gifts, and anointing is exactly what the congregation needs to grow. Not everyone who appears at your church has everyone's best interest in mind, but you do. Abraham lived a particular lifestyle because he was to become the father of many nations. You as well, live a certain lifestyle for many. Whereas some people are not thinking about the many because they only want a particular idea implemented, due to their insecurities or pride.

You can be a blessing to the masses. Indeed, Jesus was. He did bless all 5,000 people with fish and loaves. Likewise, you can have a great platform where you impact many. Yet, Jesus made sure to prioritize His time with the 12 disciples. You cannot be available all the time; Jesus was not. Sometimes He would pull away and keep moving even though people were clamoring for His attention (Mark 1:35-39). When you are always available, it appears you don't know who you are, because it seems as if you want people to define who you are. When you understand your identity and your assignment, you do not have time for everyone or everything. Jesus knew there were certain people and places He had to make time for to complete His assignment—He was purposeful. It would be best if you did the same.

You are a blessing to many people. Do not change for the few that have arrived at your church without truly honoring your position. If you adjust for the rebellious, you will betray the ones already committed to your leadership. Wherever there is a true leader, that leader will always have the best intentions for everyone. They will even make sacrifices so others can achieve. You are that kind of leader! Stay the course.

YOU ARE WORTHY

God knew why He chose the leaders He did, even if initially they did not. Jeremiah thought he was too young, Moses believed he was not eloquent in speech, Gideon thought he was not significant, Joshua was fearful, and Abraham believed he was too old. God chose David and Samson, knowing they had issues with lust. Unless you were never truly called to ministry, dear leader, you could not change the fact that God chose you.

Jeremiah felt crushed by his ministry. People were coming against him so badly that he even thought God was against him (Jeremiah 20:7). Yet, as he is pouring out in anguish before God, he cannot ignore that God is still with him. He said, "*But the Lord is with me like a mighty warrior; so my persecutors will stumble and not prevail...*" (Jeremiah 20:11a).

There are days as a leader when you will be tempted to believe the nay-sayers and criticizers. Like Jeremiah, you may even want to curse the day you were born (Jeremiah 20:14). But deep down, the leader always knows God is there. You are worthy of the ministry because God is a "warrior" within you.

This is why you must never depend on the people to define your ministry. Never equate attendance, money, fame, or giftedness as representing your relationship or ministry status with God. Remember, people were doing great signs and wonders on Christ's behalf, yet Christ said He did not know them (Matthew 7:21-23). You are doing well as long as you know God and His will for your ministry.

You will make mistakes. Notice I said mistakes and not choices. If you choose to do immoral things in your ministry, then it is time to submit yourself to the mentors or leaders in your life. You need to confess, repent, and get healed of whatever led you to make those decisions. However, even the best leaders make mistakes. Samuel almost anointed the wrong man to be king. Here is a major prophet who would have made the wrong decision had God not intervened (1 Samuel 16:6-7). God knows we are works in progress, but some people will not accept that. The truth is that some people will leave you over one mistake. While they have never had the pressure of being in your position, they will assume they are experts, depart, and talk badly about you. Misspeaking happens in a sermon, misquoting the scripture, forgetting to call someone, and arriving late a few times are all things that happen because we are human beings. Nevertheless, there is a level of excellence the visionary leader must maintain.

Mistakes will happen. Mistakes are just regular occurrences people experience. But you will have to accept that some people believe you should be flawless.

You will not only make mistakes, but you will need to take the blame for other people's decisions. Why? Because you are the one that approves everything. Therefore it all falls back on you. What makes you such a great leader is that you take chances or make faith choices that no one else would. You give people opportunities that, by human standards, may not deserve them. So when you give someone responsibility, and that person fails, people will blame you for putting that person in a position of authority. But that is what Jesus did! He made Judas an apostle and treasurer while knowing Judas would betray Him.

Should Jesus have made a different choice? Is He a bad leader because He chose Judas? Did Christ make a mistake? No, Jesus knew that Judas was necessary for His ministry. Likewise, as a leader, you know there are times when you would not put someone in leadership except that God wanted it. Ananias wanted to avoid helping the Apostle Paul receive his sight back. Because of Paul's aggressive acts towards Christians, he did not think Paul deserved prayer. But Ananias did go to Paul and pray for him to receive his sight (Acts 9:10-16). And Paul became the great apostle to the Gentiles.

As the leader, God will have you appoint people to positions, and they will fail, betray or hurt the church. Perhaps they were never supposed to defect, but God gave them a chance. They may do better next time. Sometimes only God knows why. And in His sovereignty, He allows things to happen that we cannot comprehend. And it is better that way. Because you might interfere with His perfect plan if you knew, some people would accuse you of making the wrong choice by installing an inadequate person. Other times, you will appoint others who do well, and that is always wonderful. Either outcome, you were obedient, rejoice.

PRESERVE PEOPLE

Without you, some people would have never reached the pinnacle of what God had for them. Your presence keeps people faithful and on track with God, whether it is acknowledged or not. That was the effect Moses had on the Israelites. So long as Moses was present, the Israelites did better. They won wars when Moses would lift his hands in praise toward God, and they were protected from God's wrath when Moses interceded for them (Exodus 32:11-14). However, when Moses was removed from the Israelites' presence for a long time (40 days), the Israelites decided to worship a golden calf. Their worship went to idols instead of God.

This is why the Devil works so hard to discourage you. He knows that when you are at your best, so are the people following you. Just like Moses, God uses you to preserve people! When people are confused, struggling, and about to give up, the Holy Spirit uses you to inspire, encourage, train, and elevate people. The reality is that you make a difference. Some families and individuals are better for coming in contact with the Christ in you.

God has appointed and has biblically encouraged you to check and evaluate His flock. Scripture says, "*Preach the word; be prepared in season and out of season; correct, rebuke and encourage—with great patience and careful instruction*" (2 Timothy 4:2). Unfortunately, many people do not believe pastors or fivefold ministers should correct them. No matter how gentle, sincere, and loving a leader may come across, some people are too prideful to be corrected, even if they are wrong. People will quickly leave a church the moment a pastor disagrees with them. Their pride will not allow them to need improvement. But God has anointed you for this task, and the people that submit to your leadership will be thankful as they grow.

Leading others takes a lot of time and patience, more than we initially think. As a leader, always recognize that the people you serve are God's people, not yours. Even the most difficult people matter to God. Therefore put your best into people. Do all your ministry as unto the Lord. Be faithful. There will be times when you need to rebuke, correct, and, unfortunately, excommunicate when God leads you to do so, but you could also be training the next David or Deborah. So give people space and grace to grow.

FAITHFUL PEOPLE

Jesus told a story about a shepherd who leaves the ninety-nine sheep to find the one sheep that wandered (Matthew 18:12). I love that story. The emphasis is on the faithfulness of the shepherd who goes after that one sheep. That is what Christ has done for all of us. He came and saved us from our sins. And if you love ministry more than Christ, this may be a time for you to ask Him to restore your relationship with Him or for Him to come into your life for the first time. I know of people who started in ministry and realized they were not Christians while doing ministry. They were just moral and good people preaching, teaching, and leading. This book will have done you no good apart from Christ's salvific work on the cross.

Essentially, the story is about salvation and Christ's love for His people. We all can relate to that one sheep that went astray. But what about the 99 that stayed? While this story is primarily about salvation, the 99 could also represent those Christians who, after having been saved, remain consistent in their faith and commitment. This is all to say, as the leader, be grateful for those who remain in the sheep's pen and embrace your leadership as one who represents Christ.

There will be faithful people in your ministry. Similar to Jonathan and David's relationship, there will be a mutuality between the leader and the congregation that advances what God wants to do. When Israel was given over to the pagan worship of Baal, Elijah thought he was the only prophet left, only for him to discover a man named Obadiah, who was faithful to God and hid a hundred prophets from Jezebel (1 Kings 18:4).

God will make sure to surround you with faithful people. David was a great warrior, but he also had comrades who fought alongside him (2 Samuel 23:8-39). So make sure to acknowledge those that are faithful. The Bible teaches that God will reward us for our deeds (Revelation 22:12). God does notice our contributions. Likewise, make sure to embrace and celebrate those in the church that have been exceptional. You will go far with those faithful people.

And this is how I want to end this book, by saying that God's Church has always been made up of faithful people, or we could say a people full of faith! Father Abraham was not a flawless man. But he did believe in God. His faithfulness produced more faithful people who, too, believed in God. There will always be a remnant of people wanting God's best. And just as God would raise judges to defend His people, God will always raise great leaders in the days ahead to be a light in the darkness. Keep winning, Church; we are the light of the world!

ACKNOWLEDGMENTS

Thanks to my editor, who spent hours looking over my content and was a great consultant for this book.

Thanks to all the fivefold ministers and Christian leaders who have influenced me greatly in ministry.

The highest praise and thanks to the Holy Spirit, who has always been my help!

OTHER TITLES
BY
BRIAN D. BEVERLY II

Available at Amazon.com